EASIER SAID THAN DONE

The Undeniable, Tour-Tested Truths You Must Know (and Apply) to Finally Play to Your Potential on the Golf Course

Dr. Rick Jensen
with Dave Allen

www.drrickjensen.com

Text and cover design by Beth Farrell
Text layout by Ethan Evanston
Graphs by Sea Script Company
Dr. Jensen's photograph by Lucy Unsworth

Text photographers:
p. 6: Aubrey Hart/Hulton Archive/Getty Images
p. 17: Warren Little/Getty Images Sport/ Getty Images
p. 20: Steve Powell/ Getty Images Sport/ Getty Images
p. 36: Timothy Clary/AFP/Getty Images
p.44: Augusta National/Masters Historic Imagery/Getty Images
p.51: Jamie Squire/Getty Images Sport/ Getty Images
p.57: Augusta National/Masters Historic Imagery/Getty Images
p. 69: Stephen Munday/Getty Images Sport/ Getty Images
p.78: Brick House Pictures/Ironica/Getty Images
p. 82: Stephen Munday/Getty Images Sport/ Getty Images
p.91: Rich Pilling/Major League Baseball Platinum/Getty Images
p. 102: Augusta National/Masters Historic Imagery/Getty Images
p. 108: David Cannon/Getty Images Sport/ Getty Images

ISBN: 978-0-9828663-0-6
Library of Congress Card Catalogue No.: 2010932552

Sea Script Company
Seattle, Washington

First Printing August 2010

Sea Script
SEA SCRIPT COMPANY
www.seascriptcompany.com
info@seascriptcompany.com
206.748.0345

To Rosemarie—
my wife, my confidante, my best friend
I love you.
"Family First!"

Other books by Dr. Rick Jensen:

Drive to the Top!
5 Timeless Business Lessons Learned
from Golf's Greatest Champions

available at www.drrickjensen.com

Table of Contents

Acknowledgements

I am forever grateful for the knowledge, creativity, content, and organization provided by Dave Allen. Dave's expertise as a writer, editor, and communicator made my ideas and experiences come to life in a way that I could have never created on my own.

Lorin Anderson was instrumental in this book project from start to finish. His guidance, support, direction, and tireless feedback were immeasurable, and I can't thank him enough for the contributions that he offered. Lorin's shared passion for the message and purpose of this book provided the motivation needed to stick with it to the end.

Beth Farrell went above and beyond her role as a publisher by indicating that every request, idea, and creative touch that I considered was valued and, if at all possible, was incorporated into the book layout and design. Beth's commitment to quality and service is beyond compare.

I could not have written this book were it not for all of the teachers, coaches, players, and sport science professionals with whom I have worked over the years. Were I to mention them all by name, I'd double the length of this book. Their love of the game, commitment to their students, and willingness to share their thoughts, insights, and expertise with me has been endless. I have immense respect and admiration for those teaching professionals who continue to learn, who understand what is required to coach golf, and who truly develop their students' golf skills (and not just analyze their golf swings).

I'd like to thank my parents, Barbara and Ron Jensen, for their enduring love and support. Dad introduced me to golf as a child, and Mom put up with us chipping in the living room (until we broke the window!).

Finally, I am so thankful for my family—Rosemarie, Danielle, and Connor. Their support, understanding, and encouragement, coupled with lots of hugs, laughs, and family-fun, keep me loving life each and every day.

Introduction

Imagine for a moment that you're in a boxing ring with Mike Tyson. Now, before you say, "Yeah right, Dr. Rick," you have good reason to be there: You have an opportunity to earn one million dollars if you can last a full round with the former heavyweight champion. If after three minutes in the ring with Tyson you're still standing, you're an instant millionaire.

Now, how confident do you think you would be as you entered the ring? Better yet, what do you think the chances are of you lasting those three minutes? That's right, zero! Unless Mr. Tyson is in a wonderful, giving mood or you struck a deal with him beforehand that every dollar will go to his favorite charity, you're as good as dead—or, if you're lucky, you'll just get knocked out immediately. Without the necessary boxing skills and training, you're going to be anxious, fearful, and choking your guts out. How could it be any other way?

So, why is it so likely that you'll be knocked out? Is it due to your lack of mental toughness? Your fear of failure? A poor pre-fight routine? Or your lack of positive thinking? Of course not! The reason you are going to be lying flat on your back is quite obvious—it's because you're not adequately prepared for the challenge! Whether you're in a ring with Mike Tyson or on the golf course facing a difficult shot over water, lack of preparation is the No. 1 cause of failure during competition. The mental states (e.g., anxiety, fear, negative thoughts) that accompany the situation are more often symptoms of the lack of preparation, not the cause of the failure.

How many times have you heard golfers say they have a hard time taking their game from the range to the course? Interestingly, they more often than not think the cause is "mental." The word they use most often is "choking." Their game succumbs under pressure and they automatically assume it's something mental, not physical. They never once think that their problem may be related to their skills; that they just might not be good enough.

I'll give you a perfect example: Several years ago, I met with a PGA Tour player who explained to me that he had played the Tour quite successfully for years, yet recently was struggling to make cuts. I asked him, "Why do you think you are missing cuts?" He explained that he was quite sure he was doing something wrong mentally and wanted me to help him identify and resolve the mental problem.

We headed to the course where I could watch him play, talk with him about his mental processes, and observe how he reacted to situations on the course. Amazingly, his mental approach to the game was fantastic. His pre-shot routine was spot on, his attention over the ball was perfect, his pre-swing decision-making was world-class, and his ability to manage his emotions following poor shots was excellent. In summary, his mental game was Tour-caliber. With that said, after nine holes, he was 4-over par, primarily because he wasn't hitting fairways and had missed numerous greens in regulation. In short, he wasn't controlling his ball-flight well from tee to green.

As we made the turn to No. 10, I said to him, "Is this how you've been playing out on Tour?" He said "Exactly!" I asked, "Why do you think you shot 4 over on that nine? Why do you think you're struggling with controlling your ball?" He said, "I don't think I'm doing the right things mentally." I replied, "What things?" He answered, "I don't know, that's why I came to see you."

I explained to him that his mental skills were very sharp, terrific to be honest. I said, "We've been discussing a wide range of mental aspects of your game and I have to say that everything you're doing is textbook. Your mental game seems excellent. Given that, why do you think you played as you did?" He replied, "I don't know, but you obviously have some idea as to what's going on, so what is it?" I said, "I think that your skill, not your mind, is not good enough. I'm not trying to offend you, but it's likely that your ball-control skills are just not as good as they should be; it's not necessarily a mental thing."

He adamantly disagreed with my assessment; he was sure it was mental. So I took him to the practice range so that we could eliminate the mental demands that are present on the golf course. I pointed to a green on the range and asked him: "As a Tour player, how many balls out of 10 would you expect to be able to hit on that green that is 160 yards away?" He answered, "Probably about nine." I said, "Okay, let's see." He hit three out of 10 on the green. I said, "Maybe that was a fluke, try another set." He hit four on the green.

I said, "Try one more time." Four, once again. I said, "What do you think is keeping you from hitting nine out of 10 balls on that green?" He replied, "Obviously, I must be making the same mental mistake here that I am making on the course."

This is a Tour player doing this, finding something, anything, to pin the blame on but his skill. I finally said to him, "Look, I really believe that it's your skill. You're asking me for my assessment, and I don't believe that the cause is a mental one." I then asked him, "How often do you practice?" He said, "I don't practice anymore." I said "How come?" He said, "I stopped working with my teacher two years ago and haven't had a lesson since. Anyway, if I have to practice at this point in my career, something must be wrong with me."

Unfortunately, this scenario is all too common. As sport psychology has become more mainstream in the game of golf, "I'm mental" has become the vogue excuse for lack of skill. I can't make it any clearer: More often than not, it's not mental! The fact is most golfers aren't good enough to choke. Why? Choking implies that a player has actually mastered a skill and then the skill surprisingly breaks down under pressure. The reality is that most amateur golfers haven't adequately developed a skill to a level that it is consistent and reliable even under the most comfortable of situations.

Golfers mistakenly believe that if they watch a golf tip on television, read a magazine article by a top teacher or plop down $150 bucks for a one-hour lesson, then they should play well the next time they tee it up. Let's face it, when you book a lesson with a teacher, you expect to get some kind of quick swing fix, or cure.

You want a tip that, upon your next trip to the course, will have a positive impact on your score. No way! It's not how it works. But does the instructor tell you that? Not usually. What you're not told is that it takes thousands and thousands of golf balls and months of transfer training to get rid of that slice once and for all. Rather than face the truth, you maintain a faulty expectation that the swing tip you received on Tuesday will help you keep the ball in the fairway and knock it past your friend come Saturday. It's not right.

• • • • • • • •

My goal with this book is to educate golfers about what they don't know, and how they can really get better. What you don't know is that the system in place for teaching you how to play golf is broken. There is a process to learning and applying athletic skills which involves much more than a video analysis of your golf swing, a quick lesson on the range, and wishful thinking that it will make an immediate difference on the course. If golfers truly want to get better, they have to stop blaming their failures on choking or the latest tip they received from their instructor (or a golf magazine). Instead, golfers must be told the truth—getting better at golf involves a commitment of time, resources, and effort.

The system, as it's constructed now, is set up in a way that the teacher will give you a one-hour lesson, take your money and send you off to play on the weekend, often with no discussion of how long it will take to own that skill and make it a permanent fixture in your game. It's what I like to refer to as customer-service instruction: The student gets what he or she wants (the quick fix, the split-screen video comparison to a Tour player, a DVD to take home), but not what he or she needs to make the fault go away for good (an assessment, a plan for how to get better, on-going feedback, and coaching).

Golfers don't want to hear that the reason they're not getting any better is because they don't practice, or that their expectations for what it takes to learn and to play good golf are flawed. What they want is to see their swings on video and then saved to a DVD, so they can show their pals what it is they're working on; or, as I said earlier, they want a quick fix that will cure that slice with minimal effort. Instead, what generally happens is the tip they get doesn't transfer to the course under pressure, and they wind up blaming their teacher and walking across the street to see another pro. Or they go and buy a book or read a magazine article in hopes of finding a better tip that is the magic pill they're seeking.

It doesn't make any sense, not when you consider how other sports are learned. Other sports aren't taught via magazines or in a restricted teaching area on a range; they're taught on the field of play. Skills are learned; they're not just explained. Other sports have coaches, not technique gurus who analyze the mechanics of your motion, provide a tip, and then send you on your way to test it under game conditions.

Who's to blame? Is it the golfers? They are just plugging into the existing instruction programs that are available to them. So maybe it's the media's fault? I don't think so. The media is only doing what it is designed to do—deliver information, sell magazines, inform, and entertain. Does anyone really believe that publications, the internet, or television are effective means by which to learn an athletic skill? Cost-effective, yes; effective, no! So, how about we blame the teachers? Well, teachers are simply doing what they've been trained to do (or should I say "un-trained" to do). Most teachers have little academic or applied training in the disciplines critical to building athletic skills: motor learning, coaching, biomechanics, physical fitness, sport psychology, etc. Consequently, they teach as they've been taught. They embrace a swing methodology and focus their lessons on teaching their students to swing the club the "right way."

Teachers perpetuate the age-old instruction methodology, and the public doesn't know enough to challenge the status quo. The golf industry as a whole continues to make money even if golfers aren't getting better. What is clear is that the system is in desperate need of repair. What is needed is a good dose of education—knowledge is power—and knowing what it takes to REALLY get better would benefit everyone. Chances are that if you really understood what it takes to improve and you had a qualified coach to guide you along each step of the process, you could accomplish your goals.

In this book are 12 non-negotiable, undeniable truths that you must know to learn golf and play to your potential on the golf course. Frankly, these 12 Truths are "Easier Said Than Done." Informing you of these truths is the easy part, encouraging and helping you apply them to your golf game is my ultimate goal. Different people have different reasons why they don't improve. For some, it may be that they're taking infrequent lessons but need coaching; others might not be sticking with their teacher long enough or are skipping a vital step in the skill-building process. If you read all 12 Truths you will come across one or two and say, "Whoa, that definitely applies to me." You will understand what it takes to get better, and why quick fixes are just that—quick, temporary solutions that don't hold up over time. You will stop blaming your performances on being mental, or choking, and start down the path of real improvement.

If you're hoping to wake up one day with a whole new golf game and looking for a magic elixir, then this book is not for you. If you want to go from shooting 100 to 90 or 90 to 80, there is a way to do it, and it's touched upon in these 12 Truths. It doesn't mean you have to bang 1,000 balls every day, but you're going to have to put some time in. If you have a limited amount of time to dedicate to golf, I'm going to tell you how to use that time most efficiently so you can achieve your goals.

The time for excuses is over. If you know the truth—i.e., the real reasons why you're not getting better and not playing to your potential—then you'll be armed with some very valuable information that few golfers have. You'll realize that you need to know more than just how to make a proper backswing; you will finally know what it takes to truly learn the game and play to your potential. As I've mentioned, the 12 Truths are "Easier Said Than Done," so I'll caution you now, reading this book will not on its own improve your game; you must apply the 12 Truths discussed within! Knowledge combined with action is the formula to greatness—you are on your way!

Easier Said Than Done

Truth #1

GOLF IS A GAME OF SKILL, IT'S NOT ABOUT THE SWING

Several years ago I was working with a very talented golfer who had aspirations about playing on the Champions Tour. He said to me, "Dr. Rick, I'm not on Tour because my ball-striking is very weak. My short game is phenomenal—I play with guys on Tour who wish they had my short game—but from tee to green, I'm not doing something right. Can you help me?"

I said, "Let's take a look," and so we headed out to the first tee at PGA National where, right on cue, he hit his first drive weakly onto the fairway. His second shot didn't fare much better, and wound up short of the green in some rough. Neither shot looked Tour-caliber, but that was quickly lost on me when I saw him play his third shot from just off the green. It was the most unusual pitching motion I had ever seen: He hinged the club up sharply, like he was about to kill a snake, and took a quick stab at the ball. There was nothing fluid about it, yet the ball came to rest about a foot from the hole for an easy tap-in par.

I was speechless, although that didn't stop me from asking him about his unorthodox technique as we were walking off the green. "Where did you learn how to pitch the ball?" I asked. "Your motion is quite unique."

Wrong question.

He screamed, "Darn it, here we go again. I thought you'd be different." I said, "What do you mean?" He let me have it: "You're just like everybody else. The first thing you comment on is my pitching. Why? Because you see it through a lens that doesn't fit what you expect to see. Now, you're all caught up in that. How about noticing that my tee shot barely made the fairway and I missed the green."

At that point, he reached into his bag and grabbed six balls, which he promptly chucked into a variety of difficult lies all around the green. Then he pulled out his sand wedge and said, "Come with me," and proceeded to hit every ball to within three feet of the flagstick.

"I told you when I arrived here that my short game is awesome," he said. "For you to make a comment about my pitching technique is ridiculous. Now, are you going to help me with what I came here for?"

I learned a very valuable lesson that day—do not critique a player's technique until first assessing how good he or she is. Skill is what's most important. A good-looking golf swing doesn't make you a great player; one that allows you to control the distance, direction, and trajectory of your shots does. Although Jim Furyk has a swing that resembles "an octopus falling out of a tree," as CBS commentator David Feherty once famously put it, it does get results.

No two swings on the PGA Tour are exactly the same—some are even quite unusual—but what they all share in common is an ability to control the ball. That's skill. Amateurs spend too much time on the lesson tee today trying to build a good-looking golf swing, instead of one that repeats or delivers a consistent and predictable shot pattern. We associate good golf with having a good swing, but where does that get you if that swing can't consistently produce shots that locate the fairway or the green?

Develop Your Golf Skills, Not Your Golf Swing

There is too much focus on the mechanics of the golf swing. Think about all of the top-selling instruction books out there today—*The Stack and Tilt Swing, Hank Haney's Essentials of the Swing, Ben Hogan's Five Lessons: The Modern Fundamentals of Golf, The X-Factor Swing, The Plane Truth for Golfers, The Golfing Machine, The Eight-Step Swing, Search for the Perfect Swing*—they all focus on swing technique, and how to get your body in the right positions to execute a perfect swing. They don't spend much time telling you how to bring your ball-flight down, or how to fade the ball to an elevated green with a back-right pin placement. Sure, they improve your knowledge of what it takes to strike a ball well, but they don't explain how to turn that knowledge into a habit that you can transfer to the golf course.

Now, don't get me wrong: Having a technically-sound golf swing is important, but only so if it contributes to a player being more skillful, not more technically perfect. Tour pros do work on swing technique, but they do so because it supports the development of their larger goal—ball-control (i.e., more solid contact, better directional control). Teachers need to spend more time teaching their students the skills to control the ball like Tiger Woods, not make them swing like Tiger Woods.

All other sports are skill-based: You don't see a baseball coach obsessing over the mechanics of players' hitting motions; he spends his time providing feedback to players as they work on their skills—fielding ground balls, throwing to the cut-off man, sliding into the bag, or turning double plays. The technical instruction is sprinkled in during a player's skill development practice. But not in golf: The student spends the vast majority of his 60 minutes on the lesson tee working on different positions in the swing, or having his swing broken down on video. Where's the skill training?

As I learned that one morning at PGA National, it's not about the swing, it's about controlling the ball and getting it in the hole in the fewest amount of strokes possible.

Golfers think if they shoot a high number, it's because of bad technique. They then go search out a teacher in hopes of finding a fix to remedy what ails their swing. This leap to a technical fix is not necessarily the correct response. If you're a 15-handicapper who is having a hard time breaking 90, the first thing you need to ask yourself is, "What skills am I lacking?" Are you having a hard time hitting greens? Do you miss too many fairways? How often do you get up and down from off the green? Are you three-putting much too often? To really get better, the first thing you need is an accurate prioritization of the skills in your game that cost you the most shots, not a side-by-side comparison of how your full swing stacks up against Tiger's.

There are three essential skills that will help you to lower your scores:

1. ball-control
2. decision-making
3. self-management

The most important of these skills is, by far, ball-control. If you can control the direction, distance, and trajectory of your ball consistently (i.e., move it from Point A to Point B in a predictable fashion), then you can play good golf. If you combine good decision-making (factoring in the wind, speed and slope of the greens, the lie, etc.) and self-management (controlling your emotions, managing your attention, etc.) with good ball-control skills, you can play great golf.

"The ultimate judge of your swing is the flight of the ball." –Ben Hogan

You can have good ball-control without "a picture perfect" swing. There are guys who play well on Tour with a shut clubface at the top of their swing, and others who've made a pretty successful living playing golf with an open clubface at impact (Bruce Lietzke). You have those who cross the line at the top of their swings (Fred Couples, John Daly) or take the club back to the outside and loop it inward (Jim Furyk, Lee Trevino). Jack Nicklaus had a flying right elbow, Arnold Palmer a follow-through that came to a screeching halt, and Annika Sorenstam a head-turning move that would make you dizzy, yet all of them are major champions and Hall of Famers because they could do one thing particularly well—control the golf ball.

Golf is About Controlling Your Ball

As Player Development Consultant to the WTA Tennis Tour, I've had the opportunity to attend many Grand Slam championships. One year I was sitting in a box at the U.S. Open in Flushing, New York, with a prominent tennis coach I know well and I asked him, "How come I never see you videotape any of your players to provide them feedback on their technique?"

Arnold Palmer dominated the game with a less-than-picture-perfect swing.

Well, he just about bounced me onto the court. He turned to me and said, "There you go with that golf stuff again. If you ever try to bring those golf teaching methods into the world of tennis training, I will personally make it my mission to make sure you're not welcome among the top tennis coaches." He continued: "Tennis pros understand how to make people better at tennis. We don't have to analyze every little motion to improve their game.

It's not about their motion, it's about hitting the ball where you need to hit it in the court."

Many of his friends were golf pros, so he understood how they had a tendency to slow down, stop, and freeze every motion, breaking the swing down into hundreds of pieces. He explained if he ever stopped a tennis player to think about every little position in their stroke, they'd be sunk. He then pointed to one of the women on the court—one of his pupils—and said to me, "Look at her knees. I need to get her to bend more at the knees so that she can increase the amount of topspin on her shots. She stands with her legs too straight as she hits her ground strokes and, as a result, she tends to hit a lot of fliers that carry beyond the baseline. I don't have to put that on video, show it in slow motion, and compare her to other players to prove it to her, and doing so certainly doesn't make it go away."

He then pointed out to me that when practicing with this player, he would intentionally slice the ball to avoid ever hitting a topspin shot to her. "If I were to hit topspin, the ball would jump up," he said. "This would cause her to straighten her legs and stand up as she hit the ball, not bend her knees. But when I hit a slice, the ball skids on the court and stays below her waist. She then has to bend her knees substantially to go down and get the ball. I can change her habit by controlling the way she practices."

It was his job to get his student to hit the ball with more topspin, and he didn't need to show her other pros bending their knees or spend countless hours analyzing her technique. He got the results he wanted (more topspin on her shots by bending more at the knees) simply by the way he fed her ground strokes.

Ultimately, it was about how well she controlled the ball. Golf is no different: It's not about getting your swing to look a certain way, it's about putting the ball where you intend to put it. Developing the skills to do so is the key to playing better golf, not imitating a pro's swinging motion or making your swing fit a teacher's ideal swing model.

Summary

1. Stop trying to make your swing look like a Tour pro's. Jack Nicklaus, Arnold Palmer, and Lee Trevino won many major championships with unorthodox swings. The emphasis should be on playing good golf, not having a picture-perfect golf swing.
2. Seek coaches who teach skills, not swing positions. All other sports are skill-based. If you watch a typical baseball practice, you'll see coaches teaching their players how to field a ground ball, turn a double play, or slide into second base. Only a small percentage of the time is spent on the mechanics of hitting or throwing a baseball. Too many golf lessons are spent diagnosing and fixing swing positions.
3. The three essential skills that you must master to shoot lower scores are: a) ball-control, b) decision-making, and c) self-management. Seek out a teacher who will assess and teach all three of these skills, not simply look at your swing mechanics and match them against a pre-established technical model.

Truth #2

ALL SKILLS ARE NOT CREATED EQUAL

Can you imagine how "good" a tennis player you'd be if the only skill you ever learned was how to hit a great first serve? Unless you could hit 100% of your first serves for aces, you'd have no chance. Since tennis is a game of many skills (returning serve, forehands, backhands, volleys, overheads), you cannot possibly succeed as a one-skill wonder. Yet, that's what a lot of golfers aspire to be. They are obsessed with the full swing and, in particular, how to hit the long ball off of the tee.

It's a macho factor: Most golfers want to say they were able to outdrive their playing partners come Saturday—even if every one of their pals beats them where it counts, on the scorecard.

Much of our fascination with power stems from aggressive marketing campaigns by the equipment manufacturers. You can't watch a golf telecast or pick up a golf magazine these days without seeing ads for a new, high-octane driver. "Longer," "straighter," "more forgiving than ever before," the ads proclaim. "High launch, low spin." "Our longest driver ever." More often than not, these ads are attached to the John Dalys of the game—guys known for the long ball. The temptation to demo one of these new drivers is almost impossible to resist, and that's exactly what the manufacturers are counting on. They know that if they get one of these drivers in your hands, and you hit a few towering shots with it on the range, you're buying. The driver is the one club that has no perceived limit to it (in terms of distance), and golfers are always craving more yards off the tee than they can get with their current driver. They're never satisfied.

Teachers don't help matters much. When a student comes to them for a first lesson, they'll often ask what he or she would like to work on. Chances are the student is going to say, "I'd like to hit my driver farther and straighter." And that's what he or she will spend an hour on. The teacher doesn't want to disappoint the student and say, "No, let's work on your pitching and putting instead because that's where the majority of strokes are coming from." Hoping that the student is pleased and returns for another lesson, the teacher simply gives his student what he or she asks for (a quick fix lesson), not what will really make a lasting difference (a training plan focused on the student's greatest needs).

Additionally, golfers like to work on the parts of the game that they enjoy or are good at. Consequently, they continue to further develop their strengths over time, while ignoring their weaknesses. Often, amateurs are not good at pitching or putting, because they rarely practice these skills. I can't tell you how many times I've seen an amateur hit their second shot on a par 5 to inside 80 yards of the green, and then walk away with a double bogey on the hole. Why? They don't practice their wedge game or putting. So, they skull their wedge shot over the green, chip the ball to 25 feet, and then three-putt for a double bogey.

Identify Those Skills that are Most Essential

Certain skills are more highly correlated with scoring than others. For proof of this, all you need to do is look at the individual stats of the top money winners on the PGA Tour in 2009.

2009 SEASON PGA TOUR RELATIVE RANKINGS

	Tiger Woods	Steve Stricker	Bubba Watson	David Duval
Money won	**1**	**2**	**28**	**130**
Scrambling percentage	1	2	135	183
Putts per greens in regulation	23	1	41	38
Greens in regulation	16	57	26	179
Driving distance	21	104	1	53

The top two earners on the list—Tiger Woods and Steve Stricker—also finished Number 1 and 2 on the Tour in scrambling, which is the percentage of time a player makes par or better when missing a green in regulation. That same year, the No. 1 ranked player in driving distance was Bubba Watson, who finished 28th on the money list, primarily as a result of being ranked 41st in putting and 135th in scrambling. Clearly, the ability to get the ball up and down in the short game is a bigger barometer of success than hitting the ball miles off the tee.

I'm often asked, "What happened to David Duval?" as if some mental demon mysteriously invaded the former No. 1 ranked player's game. As we discussed in Chapter 1, golf is a game of skills, and as you can see by Duval's 2009 stats, although his putting and driving distance is still competitive, he struggles with hitting greens in regulation and getting up and down on those that he doesn't. Any player who lacks these two essential skills is going to have difficulty competing at a PGA Tour level.

As you can tell from these statistics, not all skills are created equal. Driving distance, while important (the farther you hit the ball off the tee, the shorter club you'll have into the green), won't save you as many shots as being able to putt well on a consistent basis. I work with several Tour players who have relatively poor bunker skills, but this doesn't mean that we allocate all of our training time together to bunker play. Why? For one, Tour players are not in bunkers very often. Secondly, bunker play doesn't correlate with winning on Tour as much as higher priority skills such as hitting greens in regulation, total driving, putting, or scrambling. If a Tour player has a weakness in one of these four areas, it becomes the priority.

If you are a mid-handicapper, learn to keep the ball in play, putt the ball in the hole in two strokes or less, and hit your short-game shots to within 20 feet. Until you can do this, why spend your limited practice time working on flop shots, buried lies in the bunker, knock-down shots, or punching out of the trees.

> "When I left the course after a round this year, a lady told me my biorhythms were off. I told her my golf game was off." – Jack Nicklaus

At season's end of his record-setting 2000 campaign, in which he won three-fourths of the "Tiger Slam" and claimed nine PGA Tour titles overall, Tiger Woods ranked first in greens in regulation (GIR), first in total driving (a combination of driving distance AND accuracy), second in putts per GIR, and third in scrambling. He dominated the most essential skill areas and, therefore, had one of the greatest seasons in PGA Tour history.

Knowing I am a sport psychologist, golfers often tell me that they think what separates the best players on Tour from the rest lies between their ears. Amateurs often say, "Golf is 100% mental." It's just not true! Tiger Woods might demonstrate more mental toughness than his peers, but he also controls the ball better than they do. Mental toughness is not the reason Tiger ranked in the top 3 on Tour in four of the most essential skill categories. The bottom line is that he's good—he controls his golf ball! Now don't get me wrong, Tiger's mental toughness (i.e., self-management) is excellent and is the icing on his cake—but don't kid yourself, his cake is his ball-control skills, plain and simple.

What's important to know is how Tiger got so good in the months and years leading up to the 2000 season? Well, he and his coach, Butch Harmon, dissected every part of his game and worked on those high-priority skills that presented the greatest opportunity for improvement. They didn't spend their time working on what Tiger was already good at, what he liked the most, or what he or Butch just happen to read in a golf magazine the day before.

Work on the Skills that Cost You the Most Shots

I was delivering a presentation on "How Champions Train, Think and Play!" at the 2002 PGA National Teaching and Coaching Summit in Florida, and my two guest panelists were Butch Harmon and LPGA Hall of Famer Beth Daniel. I asked Butch how club players train differently from touring pros, and he said, "The people that we teach at our clubs, they only practice what they do well, because they don't want to do what [they're not] any good [at], because that's no fun. Great players, like Beth (Daniel) and these other players, they want to improve, so what they don't do well is what they spend most of their time practicing."

Greg Norman echoed the same sentiments several years earlier. Curious about his training regiment, I asked him how he allocated his practice time. His reply: "I spend the bulk of my time working on the things that cost me the most shots in competition."

Both quotes are quite important. When you have a limited time to practice—and most amateurs are lucky to get an hour or two per week to do so—you need to work on the parts of the game that are costing you the most shots.

I'll give you another example: In her book, *Golf Annika's Way,* LPGA-great Annika Sorenstam talked about the revelation she had one off-season—that her putting was preventing her from winning more majors. Annika, who kept track of a lot of skill stats on her computer, had the worst putting year of her career in 2000, averaging 30.41 strokes per round. So what did she do about it? She devoted an extra hour per day (for six weeks) to her putting that winter, working on her speed and distance control. In one drill, she'd force herself to lag 24 consecutive putts from 30 feet within a putter's length of the hole. If she missed any single putt, she had to start over.

Annika Sorenstam relied on statistical data to identify opportunities for improvement in her game.

That extra time Annika put in on the practice green paid huge dividends in 2001, as she won the first of three Kraft Nabisco Championship titles and also became the first woman to shoot a 59 in LPGA competition. She also topped the money list with more than $2 million in earnings.

Summary

1. Recognize that all skills are not created equal. Being mentally tough is nice, but if you are three-putting every green, improve your putting, not your mind. The game of golf is first and foremost about ball-control—specifically, driving the ball in play, hitting as many greens in regulation as possible, putting consistently well, and chipping and pitching it close to the hole.
2. Stop working on what you enjoy and start working on what skills cost you the most strokes.
3. Have your coach conduct a skills assessment of your game. A good coach should be able to look at your overall game and give you a complete assessment as to what skills need the most improvement. Ask him or her to give you a relative handicap for each of your essential skills compared to your overall handicap. For example: If you're a 15-handicapper, it is possible that your driving skills are as good as a 10-handicap, yet your putting may be at a 20-handicap level. Improve those skills that are above your overall handicap.

Truth #3

YOU CAN'T SKIP STEPS OR YOU'LL TRIP AND FALL

Most golfers think they can bypass the steps necessary to get better at a particular skill. They think there's a quick fix for everything, a magic pill that will suddenly make their slice or topped shot disappear when the weekend arrives. But it's more wishful thinking than anything else. Like other sports, there's a hierarchy of skills—a progressive set of skills in golf that you must develop over time. You have to engage in a process of learning, of truly mastering these skills.

In this chapter, I will identify the four steps to mastery. Skip any one of them, and you'll have little chance reaching the level of consistency you desire. Now, I know what you're thinking: Four steps, how about one? But think about it, how many times have you attempted to short-cut the learning process in golf by looking for the quick fix, only to find yourself right back at square one?

Interestingly, in most other sports, athletes acknowledge that quick fixes can be hazardous to one's progress, if not their physical health. Let me demonstrate what I mean. Let's say it was your desire to learn how to execute a flip on a balance beam: What would the process be for learning how to do that? Surely, you wouldn't walk into a gymnastics academy on day one and get videotaped performing your best flip. An instructor wouldn't show a video of your ill-attempted flip side-by-side with that of an Olympic gymnast just to demonstrate why you fell on your head. Such an approach to learning would not only be extremely dangerous, it would be considered malpractice on the instructor's part.

It took years for Olympic gold medalist Mary Lou Retton to master this flip.

In gymnastics, the first thing the instructor would do is give you a physical assessment to see if you're even capable of maintaining your balance on a 4-inch wide beam or doing a flip just on the ground. If you were unable to complete a flip on the ground, you certainly wouldn't get on a beam to learn it; the instructor may first put you on a trampoline using a harness for assistance.

Once you exhibit the ability to flip on the trampoline, you would move to the floor. Once you could complete a flip on the floor, you'd then learn to flip on a 4-inch line on the floor, then on a beam on the floor, and then finally on a raised beam used in competition.

This is how a qualified gymnastics instructor would train you. He or she would build upon a hierarchy of motor skills, from the simple to the more complex, gradually moving you through a multi-month, if not multi-year, process until you reached a point where you were comfortable doing a flip in competition, with an audience watching you. Now, for some of us, we'd never reach this end goal—we may decide that the task is just too demanding.

I would argue that the mechanics of hitting a golf ball are equally as complex as the mechanics of doing a flip—just ask a trained gymnast to hit a golf ball 175 yards off a tight fairway lie onto a green. But you would never expect someone to just show up at a gymnastics meet and perform a flip on the balance beam. You'd think that person was nuts! Unfortunately, that's what happens every week on the golf course. People just show up on Saturday or Sunday thinking they have a chance to succeed because of the lesson they had on Wednesday, or because of the tip they read in a magazine over their lunch break on Thursday.

It's perplexing why golf instruction isn't held up to the same standard as other sports, like gymnastics. One reason why is because you're not likely to get hurt attempting to hit a golf ball, like you would be attempting a flip on a balance beam. This lack of a significant negative consequence (i.e., injury) for teaching malpractice allows the golf industry to perpetuate the myth that golf, unlike other sports, can be learned via quick tips, magazine articles, periodic one-hour lessons, and other wishful-thinking methods. The reality is that there are negative consequences—your lack of real, sustainable improvement and an ensuing deterioration in your belief that you can get better.

Walk Your Skills Up the Four Steps to Mastery

Learning golf is a process, not an epiphany. You have to walk an athletic skill up several steps before you can master it. You can't acquire skill through the media (magazines, books, television), by sharing tips among friends, or through infrequent and disconnected lessons by a variety of teaching professionals. What other sports are learned this way? Only in golf would you attempt to flip on a balance beam before you learned to walk on the beam.

In order to finally own a skill to a point where it will hold up under pressure, you must walk the skill up "The Four Steps to Mastery."

On Step 1, you determine which skill is costing you the most strokes, seek understanding of what you're doing wrong, and identify what you need to do to fix it. Take a lesson from a golf instructor and most likely you will find yourself on Step 1—gaining an understanding of cause and effect—identifying the causes of the errors in your game and their respective solutions.

Let's say, for the sake of argument, that you have a tendency to leave your bunker shots in the sand or skull them over the green. In Step 1, your golf coach might explain to you what the bounce of

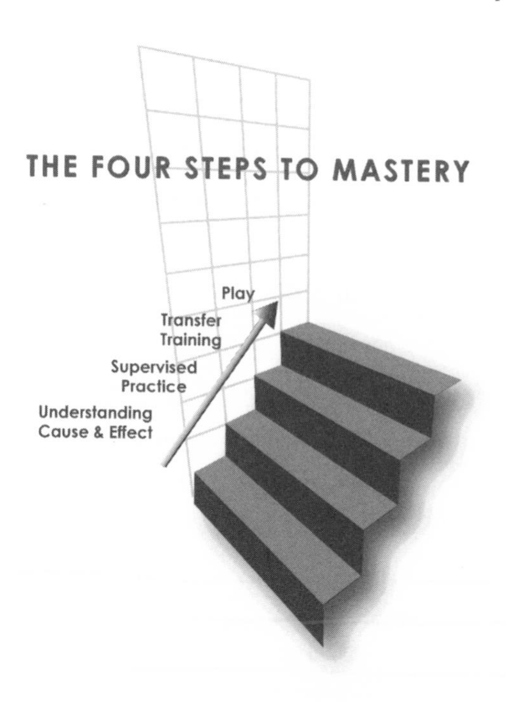

your sand wedge is, and how it's designed to work. He or she may then explain to you that your clubhead is bottoming out too soon, which is causing you to hit your shots fat and thin. Then your coach would prescribe a fix such as keeping your weight more forward (on your front foot) and a drill to help you control your entry point into the sand.

However, just because you understand what causes your poor bunker shots and how to fix them, it doesn't mean you'll be able to apply this knowledge on the golf course when it counts. To truly own the new bunker skill, you must train the skill through the next three steps.

Step No. 2 involves supervised practice—lots of repetition with feedback. Golf is a motor skill and therefore requires repetition of motion for the motor cortex of the brain to store the skill as a habit.

In our bunker example, your coach might draw a line in the sand and teach you to use it as feedback as you attempt to control: 1) the entry point into the sand and 2) the amount of sand you displace. Your coach may teach you how to get the clubhead to enter the sand at the line and to exit a defined distance after the line. Once you could do this eight times out of ten, your coach would then instruct you to place a ball two inches in front of the line, and strive to hit eight out of ten balls within a certain distance of a pin. Step 2 involves focused repetition with feedback provided by your coach (or from a drill or other training aid prescribed by the coach).

"The player who expects a lesson to 'take' without subsequent practice just isn't being honest with himself or fair to his professional." –Gary Player

The next logical step (Step 3) involves transfer training: exposing the skill to conditions that simulate those that you'd experience on the golf course under competition. Can you do the above drill eight times out of ten from a hard-packed lie or from very soft, fluffy sand? How about from a downhill lie? What about when people are watching? It is very common, when your technique is first exposed to these various transfer conditions, to revert back to your prior tendencies. Many repetitions under transfer conditions are needed to extinguish old habits and to develop the new skill to the point where it will reliably show up on the golf course. This step might take you months to transcend and is the one step that most golfers fail to complete. As players experience periodic setbacks in performance on the golf course, they often conclude that what they were working on does not work. Discouraged, they abandon Step 3, drop back down to Step 1, and then start searching for another quick fix. What you have to understand is that while it takes time, discipline, and stick-to-itiveness, transfer training is a necessary, non-negotiable step to taking a new skill to the course.

The final step (Step 4) involves playing with that skill while keeping score on the course. As with all sports, the application of the learned motor skill is what's most critical for success. Shooting a basketball in a game of horse is quite different than shooting one in an actual game with a hand in your face and the shot clock ticking down toward zero. In golf, you must learn to apply your new skill under real playing conditions, not just in a controlled environment on the practice range. This means executing your new bunker technique in competition, where you may be confronted with a high lip or a downhill lie, or where there may be water on the other side of the green. It involves decision-making (knowing how much green you have between you and the flag, and how the ball will react once it lands on the green) and self-management (keeping your focus on the shot at hand when you know water looms on the other side of the green). A skill is not completely learned until it can be drawn upon and successfully utilized on the course under competition.

"Fortunately" Learning Takes Time

I was playing golf with my brother-in-law one Saturday afternoon and he was going along quite nicely until he unfortunately chunked a rather simple pitch shot. He let out this big "ahhhhh" and I said, "What's wrong?" He said, "Corey Pavin." I asked, "What?" He then explained that he had watched Corey Pavin giving a tip on pitching the night before on Golf Channel, and he decided he'd try it. He figured that if the tip was coming from Corey Pavin, it would have to be good. I said, "You're kidding me, right?"

He wasn't. My brother-in-law made the common mistake of skipping Steps 2 and 3 (supervised practice and transfer training), and figured he could take this new knowledge right to the course and execute it. Unfortunately, it's what most golfers do: Skip from Step 1 directly to Step 4. They get a tip from a friend, a television show, or a magazine, and head to the course and give it a try! Then when it doesn't work, they blame the tip, fall back to Step 1, and start looking for another tip. If you read or hear something one night and go out the next day and try it, expecting to succeed without practicing (and transferring) the skill, you are engaging in wishful thinking!

One champion who never skipped any skill-building steps was former World No. 1 professional tennis player Ivan Lendl, who won eight Grand Slam singles titles between 1984 and 1990. During a conversation that I had with Lendl, he clarified what he thought separated the best from the rest—their willingness to stick with the learning process. Lendl explained that "fortunately" for him the process of learning a new skill takes time, and because it takes so long, not everyone will do it.

Lendl spoke of five steps, not four, that he used to build a skill to the point that it would hold up under the pressure of competition.

"It takes a long time and there are five steps to it," he said. "Step No. 1: You have to identify and decide how you are going to go about it. Step No. 2: You have to do it in practice. Step No. 3: You have to do it in a match. Step No. 4: You have to do it in a match under pressure—meaning four-all, break point in the final set. And Step No. 5: You have to do it in a big match under pressure—meaning five-all, fifth-set tiebreaker in the U.S. Open finals. It took me between 12 and 24 months, which is a long, long time to work on something before you become comfortable with it. Fortunately, from my point of view, it takes that long, because I had the desire to keep working on it and believe in my coach and myself that we were working on the right thing. A lot of guys, they just give up after three months and they stay at the level they are."

Summary

1. Stop thinking that just because you understand what you are doing wrong and how to fix it, that you can head directly to the course and execute it. Since you've skipped two critical learning steps (i.e., supervised practice and transfer training), success is unlikely.
2. Ask your coach for supervised practice sessions and on-course transfer lessons. If you can't afford multiple lessons, ask your coach to provide you with drills, training aids, and on-course activities that will develop your skills when you are practicing on your own.
3. Ask your coach to prescribe a training plan for all four steps (Understanding Cause and Effect; Supervised Practice; Transfer Training; Play). Your coach can and should play a role in all four steps.
4. Understand that you are not going to acquire a new skill overnight. It takes time to get rid of your slice or a bladed bunker shot. Just because you're not seeing results right away doesn't mean that what you are working on is wrong. Instead, it is likely that you haven't mastered the skill, that you haven't learned it yet. Keep your expectations real, plan for the long-term, and walk your skills up the Four Steps to Mastery.

Truth #4

YOU MUST STICK TO SOMETHING LONG ENOUGH TO MASTER IT

In today's society, people are accustomed to getting things faster than ever before, whether it be booking a trip on the internet, or having food prepared and delivered to their homes. We love texting and instant messaging each other because the responses come mere seconds after we hit the send button. We want our news fast, our mail delivered faster, and our transactions to be completed as quickly as possible. As a result, we've become a very impatient society. We get upset when we have a slow internet connection, whereas years ago, people patiently waited for their parents to get done with the newspaper so they could read the front-page news, sports section, or comics. We thought search engines were vehicles that the fire department used, not something that would provide us with immediate answers to all of our pressing needs.

Because people are accustomed to getting what they want faster, their expectations as golfers are that the lessons they received on Tuesday or Wednesday will translate into lower scores come

Saturday or Sunday. When they read a tip in a golf magazine that says they need to "turn their knuckles down" to hit a draw, they fully expect to see their slice turn into a draw the next time they play. If it doesn't work, then they dismiss it as bad information and either give up on learning the skill entirely or go seek another opinion.

Sometimes this search for an alternative quick fix leads golfers down another road—the road to "buy a game!" The golf industry has made millions of dollars off of golfers who want desperately to believe that they can pick up another 20 yards on their drives just by purchasing a new driver, or that they will sink more putts if they would simply buy that putter used by their favorite touring pro. Why do people never have the time to build a game, but always seem to have the cash to buy one—or so they believe?

Each year, I travel the country conducting seminars at golf clubs. Not long ago, just before I was about to address a room full of members at a club, the head pro pulled me aside and asked, "Dr. Rick, are you going to do that bit on sticking with something long enough to master it?" I said, "Yes, I intend to." He said, "You know, I'm glad that you are going to explain to my members why they should stick with one teacher and one methodology, but can I make one request?" I said, "Certainly!" He continued, "You know how you also explain why they should stick with their golf equipment as well—can you please exclude that part today?" I asked "Why?" He responded, "Because I've convinced my members that buying a new set of clubs each year is a good thing, and if you tell them to stick with their existing set, you will be taking quite a bit of money out of my pocket!"

Now I highly recommend that players get fitted for a set of clubs and invest in equipment that is right for them, but this shouldn't happen because it brings money to the pro, the fitter, or the manufacturer. Fitting should be for performance gains, and it's simply not necessary to buy a new set of clubs every year.

The Trait of Champions: Stick-to-itiveness

Most amateur golfers mistakenly believe that once they know what is wrong with their game and how to fix it, they should be able to immediately take it to the course. Not true! You are not going to develop a new skill—such as learning how to draw the ball—overnight. Walking a new skill through the four-step process in our discussion of Truth #3 may take months—even longer. You must avoid the temptation to abandon the learning process when you don't see immediate results. This improvement delay doesn't mean that what you're doing is wrong or a waste of time; more likely, it means you haven't given it enough time.

Physical skills are learned through repetition of motion. Learning any skill, like driving a car or walking, takes time. You didn't learn those skills in a day. You drove on a dead end or less-traveled street before you proceeded to the highway, and you crawled for months before you could walk. Physical skills aren't learned just through the knowledge you gain. Like any other sport you played as a kid, you got better at it over time as you practiced and applied the skill. Golf is no different. You have to train your body to repeat and execute new skills under a range of ever-changing conditions. Doing so takes time.

Arnold Palmer is an example of somebody who understood that learning takes time. I was doing a seminar one day at Bay Hill Club & Lodge in Orlando and Mr. Palmer was gracious enough to come in and answer several questions for those in attendance. I asked him, "How many teachers have you had over your career?" And he explained that his only teacher was his dad, Milfred J. (Deacon) Palmer, who worked as a golf professional and course superintendent at Latrobe Country Club outside of Pittsburgh. I then asked him if he had ever flirted with the idea of taking lessons from another teacher, and he adamantly said, "No!" Mr. Palmer went on to state that his dad taught him the greatest lesson he ever learned in golf, and that was to "stick with something long enough to master it."

Mr. Palmer explained that while other players were busy searching for a swing that would make them a master, he understood that his job was to master what his father taught him—through hard work, practice, and execution. This stick-to-itiveness that Arnold Palmer addressed is something all of the great champions possess. They have the patience to follow through with something long enough to make it a habit. They know that building a skill takes time, and rather than run at the first sign of trouble or lack of progress, they work even harder to achieve their goals.

Even into his 70s, Mr. Palmer worked on his game with his dad's methodology in mind. After his father had passed away, I saw Mr. Palmer on the range getting what appeared to be a lesson from Jim Deaton, Bay Hill's former Director of Golf. Later that day, I said to Jim, "I didn't know that you were Mr. Palmer's teacher. What was it you and he were working on?" Jim replied, "I'm not his teacher. His only teacher was his dad. I was simply giving him feedback." Jim went on to explain that at times when Mr. Palmer would head to the range to practice, he would ask Jim to accompany him to serve as another set of eyes. Jim said, "Mr. Palmer has one way he likes to swing a golf club and he knows what it is. While he's hitting balls, he'll turn to me and say, 'Can you tell me if my club is getting to this position in my backswing?' My job is to provide him feedback as to whether he is doing what he tells me he wants to be doing with his swing."

Arnold Palmer understood the importance of sticking to something long enough to master it. The results of his stick-to-itiveness speak for themselves. Do you stick with your coach, your swing methodology, your practice drills long enough to achieve mastery?

"Golf tips are like aspirin. One may do you good, but if you swallow the whole bottle, you will be lucky to survive." –Harvey Penick

Let me share another example of stick-to-itiveness with you. Years ago, I had the wonderful opportunity to teach a joint golf clinic with the late, Canadian professional Moe Norman, acknowledged by many golf pros as the greatest ball striker they'd ever seen. Moe was renowned for being a very eccentric character and for his unique 10-finger grip and one-plane golf swing. Following our clinic, I asked Moe, "How many teachers have you had throughout your career?" Moe answered, "None, I couldn't afford one." I then asked, "Given what you know now about how successful you've been, if you could do it all over again, and you had the financial resources, would you hire a teacher?" He responded, "Definitely!" Surprised by his answer, I asked, "Why would you, when your self-taught method has been so successful?" Moe said, "Yeah, but you don't realize how long it took me to become this good. Had I seen a teacher, I would have gotten here much faster. But I will tell you this, I wouldn't do it the way golfers do it today." I asked, "What do you mean?" He explained: "In my day, players married their teachers. Today, everyone is running around cheating on their teachers and having affairs!" Moe Norman understood the value of sticking with one methodology and mastering it.

Lasting Improvement May Be a Multi-Year Process

After his historic 12-shot dismantling of the field at the 1997 Masters, what did Tiger Woods do for an encore? He changed his swing! That's right, after a season in which he led the PGA Tour in money and won his first major, he and his coach, Butch Harmon, felt he could be even better. You see, that same year, Tiger finished 2nd in scoring average, 4th in greens in regulation, and 9th in total driving, and when you are as driven as Tiger, these numbers are screaming "opportunity for improvement." The media and golfing public had a hard time understanding why Butch would fix something that in their minds wasn't broken, and the criticism reached a fever pitch when Tiger won just once on Tour in 1998 and slipped to fourth on the money list.

TIGER WOODS' RELATIVE PGA TOUR RANKING 1997 TO 2000

	1997	1998	1999	2000
Annual Earnings	1st	4th	1st	1st
Scoring Average	2nd	2nd	1st	1st
Greens in Regulation	4th	30th	1st	1st
Total Driving	9th	14th	1st	1st

But did Tiger give in to what other people were saying? No, he stuck with the lesson plan that he and Butch had agreed upon even though the numbers—and victories—weren't up to the standards we know Tiger expects of himself. In 1998, Tiger's greens in regulation ranking fell to 30th and his total driving rank fell to 14th, but he never lost sight of the goal, which was to improve his distance control with his irons and his driving accuracy.

Tiger handled each inquiry about his swing with calm, saying after each tournament that his game was "getting closer" to where he and Butch wanted it. The media grew increasingly skeptical, but Tiger obviously knew what he was talking about because in 1999 and 2000, he won 17 times, including the final three majors in 2000. Woods led the Tour in GIR and total driving both seasons, and in the ultimate testament to his consistency, shot under par in all 20 PGA tournament starts in 2000 and surpassed his next closest

Upon winning the 2001 Masters, Tiger Woods became the first player in history to hold all four major titles at one time.

competitor on the money list (Phil Mickelson) by more than $4 million.

Woods is proof that it takes time to learn a skill—or, in his case, a new swing. The skill is not mastered overnight, and if it takes Tiger Woods several years to master a few swing changes, how long do you think it's going to take you to overhaul a particular skill?

Summary

1. Understand that building skill takes time—more than you think. This tough reality doesn't make it any less true. Stop trying to find a short-cut; give yourself time to improve.
2. Stop tinkering with different swing methodologies. Find a coach that you like and stick with him or her; don't abandon your coach just because the results aren't happening fast enough. Many greats of the game demonstrated stick-to-itiveness with their own coaches—Arnold Palmer with his father, Jack Nicklaus with Jack Grout, and Annika Sorenstam with Henri Reis. Sticking to an approach is more important than the approach itself.
3. Make sure to get fitted for your equipment and, as is the case with your teacher, stick to your clubs long enough to become accustomed to the length, lie, shaft flex, swing weight, etc. Avoid the temptation to go shopping for a game.

Truth #5

THERE'S NO WAY AROUND IT, PRACTICE IS A MUST

Showing up 30 minutes prior to your tee time and hitting a few balls on the range does not qualify as practice. It qualifies as a warm-up. Practice is more deliberate. It's an intentional effort—ideally, with feedback—to develop better ball-control skills, decision-making skills, and self-management skills.

When you see a player on the range working with a coach, and they're trying to minimize the hook spin on the golf ball by getting the clubhead to be less closed (or shut) at the top of the swing, that's practice. When you strive to sink 40 out of 50 putts from 8 feet without hitting the edges of a putting track that your coach has asked you to use (to prevent your path from swinging in-to-out), that's practice. Hitting 10 drives and a dozen 7-irons in the 15 minutes prior to your tee time is not practice.

More often than not, golfers will utilize their pre-round warm-up time to work on something mechanical in their golf swings. I would argue that this is the worst time to try to improve your swing because you're not going to get enough repetitions completed during that 15 or 20 minutes to create any lasting change in your skill. You don't want to head to the first tee caught between a new swing thought that creates a draw (yet not consistently) and an old swing pattern that produces a push-slice. Where will you aim? Being stuck between two ball-flights is a recipe for disaster! Often when you work on your swing prior to play, you bring a lot of unsolved questions and doubts with you to the course because the changes haven't yet become habit, and thus, you often question which ball-flight will show up and when.

Practice is golf's dirty word—no one wants to say it, and most do their best to avoid it. When I first entertained the idea of writing this book, I put together a proposal for a book publisher. One of the chapters in my outline was titled, "Practice, Practice, Practice," which elicited a phone call from my book agent. He said, "Rick, what's this chapter on practice?" I said, "It's pretty self-explanatory, it's a chapter explaining the importance of practice and how to practice effectively." He replied, "Take it out." I said, "Why?" He said, "Because nobody is going to buy anything involving practice. People don't want to practice." I said, "I can't take it out—practice is essential to getting good at golf—it has to be part of the book." So, my agent asked, "Can't you call it anything besides practice?"

I thought about it for awhile and said, "Well, the other working title I had for that chapter was *Put in the Work*." He said, "Oh no, you can't say 'work.' In no way am I going to be able to sell a book prescribing work. Try a different title." I said, "Well, what do you think about *Focused Repetition with Feedback*?" He asked, "What does that mean?" I said, "Basically, it means practice." He responded, "I love it!" Laughing, I asked, "Why?" He said, "Because I didn't know what you were referring to and neither will anyone else—it sure beats using the word 'practice.'"

Practice, Practice, Practice!

Golfers' practice habits (or lack thereof) are likely the number one reason why they do not improve. A teacher will give you a golf lesson, take your money, and send you on your way without any prescription of how much to practice or how to transfer what you were working on during the lesson to the golf course. Not that anyone complains—golfers want to get better with as little work as possible, so the notion of improvement without practice is what clearly sells in golf today.

By not telling you that practice is a must, teachers only perpetuate the idea that when something you are working on doesn't transfer to the golf course quickly, it must be wrong. What the teacher should be saying is, "It's not wrong, you just never learned it because you never practiced it."

Golf is a sport that requires practice to develop a skill, to create a new habit. It requires motor programming and, hence, a lot of repetition. According to a landmark study of elite musical performers conducted in 1993 by Dr. K. Anders Ericsson, entitled "The Role of Deliberate Practice in the Acquisition of Expert Performance," it takes 10 years of intense training (or approximately

10,000 hours of practice) for performers to compete and win competitions on the international level. Now, I'm not saying it's going to take you 10 years to get rid of your slice, but it is going to require some effort on your part.

Learning an athletic skill is not as simple as understanding and recalling what you are suppose to do. There's a difference between learning an athletic skill and learning a piece of information that is required in school. You can learn how to solve a math problem in one day, because this involves cognitive learning, not motor learning. But if your teacher tells you that you need to keep your right hand more under the shaft at the top of the backswing, it doesn't mean your body can do it the next time you play. You have to take that piece of information, turn it into a motor program that is stored in the brain, and then be able to retrieve it and send it to the muscles at will on the course. This learning process takes thousands and thousands of repetitions. It's not as simple as understanding what you are supposed to do and then deciding to do it.

"Practice puts brains in your muscles." –Sam Snead

People don't want to hear that they have to perform these repetitions. The real reason they don't get any better is because they never fully learn what they were attempting in the first place. Maybe they tested it a few times with their pro on the range, but they didn't store it in their brain. It didn't become part of their athletic repertoire, their motor system. That requires work!

Getting Good Requires Sacrifice

Vijay Singh's work ethic is legendary. Tales of him working on his game from sun up to sun down are as commonplace as Hollywood gossip. I know this because as I was setting up at daybreak for a golf school on the range at TPC Sawgrass a few years ago, Vijay was already out there hitting balls. He traversed the entire range as he practiced, going from the teeing ground to the rough to the trees to down in the practice bunkers. All morning this went on.

I headed to lunch with our group, and when we returned, Vijay was still out there. That afternoon, I headed to the course with the group to play and then returned to the range to clean up at day's end. Guess who was still there? Now, it's possible that Vjiay went out and played nine or 18 holes, but the fact that he was practicing from dawn to dusk was impressive. As we were returning the carts to the barn, I asked several of the staff in there if they had any idea how many balls Vijay hit on an average day. One of them raised his hand and said, "I do—2,000!" I clarified, "2000? How do you know that?" Proud to prove his point, the attendant pointed to a slew of empty mesh bags piled up along one of the walls and said, "Do you see those bags over there? Those are for Vijay. Each one of them holds 100 balls, and when Vijay is in town I need to have 20 of them filled. At the end of a practice day, Vijay returns 20 empty bags and it's my job to refill them."

Could you imagine yourself hitting 2,000 balls per day? Most PGA Tour players don't go to that extreme, but Butch Harmon,

Ben Hogan was renowned for his work ethic and his belief that "the secret's in the dirt."

Tiger's former coach, told me that Tiger would go through about 1,200 balls in a practice day. Greg Norman, another famed ball-beater, told me that the reason why he engaged in such a rigorous fitness program wasn't to increase his driving distance (as many amateurs believe), but it was so that his body could keep up with the physical demands of practicing from sun up to sun down.

Now, obviously, you don't have the time to devote to practice that these players do. Playing golf is what they do for a living. But the great players of the game sacrifice other opportunities in favor of making time for practice. Case in point: Following the presentation ceremony for the 2002 Solheim Cup, I was walking with a few members of the victorious United States team. We were headed for the shuttle that would transport us back to the hotel, where we could get cleaned up for the post-tournament parties that players, caddies, and coaches from both teams enjoyed.

On my way out, I spotted Terry McNamara, Annika Sorenstam's caddie, on the practice range. The Cup had concluded a couple of hours earlier and the range had been practically stripped bare, but there was Terry with Annika's bag and a teaching basket full of golf balls. I ran down the hill and said to Terry, "What are you doing?" He replied, "Waiting for Annika." I said, "She's likely on her way back to the hotel—you do know that there are activities scheduled there, don't you?" He said, "Yes, I know, but I'm supposed to meet her here." I asked, "Did you talk to her, because I'm concerned she's on the way back to the hotel and you'll be sitting here waiting a long time." He confidently said, "I didn't speak with her, but I'm sure she'll meet me here. It's still light out. We have a rule: If we have a morning tee time, we practice until dark. It doesn't matter if it's the first round of a regular tournament, a major championship, or the conclusion of the Solheim Cup. We practice. She won't be heading to any parties; she'll be coming here."

Now, that's dedication. It also shows you how disciplined the great players are with regard to their practice routines. Here was a player at the very top of her sport, and she knew full well that if she wanted to stay there she had to practice. Those players who embrace practice—like Annika, Vijay, and Tiger—do it better than anybody else, and that's what separates them from the other athletes in their sport. Imagine how much separation you could create between you and your competition if you would apply the same level of discipline and sacrifice.

Summary

1. Understand that in order to improve your skills (i.e., hit more fairways, make more putts) you have to practice. You can't just grasp the information you received from your coach or you read in a magazine article and expect it to show up on the course.
2. Recognize that trying out the tip you received days earlier on the range 30 minutes prior to teeing off is not practice. During warm-up, simply do that—warm up, identify what your ball-flight tendency is, and play it. If you don't like the ball-flight that you have, set aside time after the round or on another day to practice.
3. Block out several hours each week to practice. The more you practice, the faster you will improve and reach your goals. Why take a lesson if you're not going to take the time to practice? It would be like receiving a prescription from your doctor and not taking the medication when you get home.
4. After meeting with your coach, ask him or her to show you what to practice—and how. Ask your coach to write out the "training prescription" that you should follow until your next session, just as your doctor would.

Truth #6

WHERE LESSONS DON'T WORK, COACHING DOES

Take a moment and recall a sport, other than golf, that you played as a youngster: Football, basketball, baseball, tennis, gymnastics, field hockey, soccer, any sport. How did you learn that sport? What was the process that you engaged in to get better? Chances are you attended structured practices during which a coach provided you with instruction, feedback, and drills. Furthermore, your coach was likely present on game day to provide additional guidance to help you execute in competition what you were working on in practice.

Unlike other sports, golf is taught, and thus learned, differently—instruction is obtained via lessons (or golf schools) provided by teachers, not coaches (with the exception of high school or college teams). During a typical golf lesson, a teacher delivers knowledge about what you are doing wrong and how you can fix it (see Truth #3, Step 1: Understanding Cause and Effect). While this first step is a critical and necessary part of the skill-building process, by itself, it falls far short if the goal is to learn to play golf. Lessons alone assume that students have the ability to walk themselves through all of the steps to mastery. This flawed assumption is exactly why coaches in other sports do much more than provide lessons.

Knowledge of Cause and Effect is Not Enough

Teachers in golf too often park themselves on Step 1, and in doing so, have become experts at fulfilling the goals of this step—assessing a player's swing mechanics, identifying faults and fixes, explaining ball-flight laws, providing models of correct motion, helping students clarify their concepts, etc. However, as they've become proficient cause and effect gurus, golf teachers have neglected the other three steps required to fully master a skill.

As I've pointed out, learning a motor skill involves more than just knowing what is wrong and how to fix it. It requires continuous feedback and training over time—supervised practice, both on the course and off. Teachers should be helping students transfer skills from the range to the course, make correct on-course decisions, and manage their thoughts, their attention, and their emotions under competition. Coaches do this, teachers do not!

Instead of coaching golfers to develop the various skills needed to shoot lower scores, most teachers offer quick fixes and pointers that provide instant gratification, but minimal long-term gain. Why? Because that's what sells in today's society. We want quick fixes and immediate gains with minimal effort. If it's going to take weeks or months—or even longer—to shed those unwanted strokes from our game, we'll try and come up with another solution that won't take nearly as long.

A teacher disseminates knowledge. He or she doesn't follow you home to make sure you employ that knowledge. The teacher gives a lesson, and that's where it ends. A coach, on the other hand, makes sure that the lessons you learn in Step 1 transfer to the field of play, in a pressure environment. The coach is with you every step of the way in the skill-building process—disseminating knowledge, providing feedback during practice, overseeing your transfer training on the course, and providing additional insights while you play.

> "I think it's real important to take a student on the golf course—see how they think, see what their course management is, see how their swing reacts on the golf course." –Beth Daniel

A coach is there to push the development of a skill up all the required steps, which is what is required to completely learn a skill. A coach tells you when it's time to progress to the next step of development. A coach decides which transfer conditions (e.g., varying lies, pin locations, wind, distractions, pressure) to add to your training as you strive to take the skills you developed in practice onto the course.

Coaching is Essential to Learning Golf

Think back to when you were in Little League or playing Pop Warner football as a kid. You typically had more than one coach around to oversee your development. You might have had a parent-coach who specialized in hitting or pitching, or another who taught you how to field ground balls and run the bases properly. In football, maybe you had separate coordinators for both offense and defense. Chances are there were a number of parent-coaches around to teach you how to play the game.

Now consider what happens in the professional sporting ranks. Your typical NFL team has a quarterbacks coach, a running backs coach, a wide receivers coach, an offensive line coach, and an offensive coordinator. And that's just on the offensive side of the ball. What about your average Major League Baseball team? In addition to the manager, they have a bench coach, a first- and third-base coach, a pitching coach, a hitting coach, and just maybe another advisor or two. The salaries of these coaches stretch into the millions of dollars.

Why spend all of that money on professional coaching? Because coaching is essential to achieving results in sports! Even at a professional level, where athletes are already quite competent, coaches play a critical part in the learning process—analyzing strengths and weaknesses, customizing training programs, delivering instruction, overseeing practice, providing on-going feedback, and facilitating transfer.

High-priced coaches are not limited to team sports, however. Pro tennis coaches are paid not only to work with their players when they are practicing at home, but also to travel with their players to tournaments big and small. And the coaches stick around for the entire tournament; they don't just give a lesson or two and then pack their bags and head home. It's the same in skiing, figure skating, gymnastics, wrestling and most other individual sports—the coaches are present throughout the entire learning process. They're able to provide instruction and feedback to their athletes as they learn, play, and compete.

In golf, the teacher is largely absent from the learning process. Even on the professional level, teachers have traditionally shown up to only a few tournaments per year, usually the majors. They do not spend as much time as coaches in other professional sports overseeing their player's practice and helping transfer skills to competition. Even at a Tour level, most teachers are not coaches. But that is changing rapidly.

Phil Mickelson is often accompanied by his coach, Butch Harmon, during practice rounds.

Tiger Woods, Phil Mickelson, and a few other players are beginning to challenge this flawed paradigm. Today, these elite players contract with their coaches to do much more than show up on the range and provide a swing tip or two. Their coaches do provide lessons, but they also spend significant time off of the lesson tee providing supervised practice and on the course training.

Additionally, it is not uncommon to see these top coaches at PGA Tour events walking practice rounds with their players and observing them in the heat of battle. Tiger and Phil understand that coaching is essential.

Now, compare the coaching on the PGA Tour with what we see occurring at country clubs every day. Teachers stand on the lesson tee and give 8-10 one-hour lessons per day. Once in a while they wander over to the short game area to give a putting or pitching lesson. They rarely give playing lessons, hardly ever supervise their players' practice, and once in a blue moon observe their players compete.

To be fair, golfers are not lined up at the "coaching" door demanding more from their teachers. Instead, they fall in line, book a lesson, and later blame the pro for the fact that the lesson didn't work. Minimal effort results in minimal gain—why are we surprised?

Don't Book a Lesson, Hire a Coach

Booking a lesson with a teacher is the typical course of action taken by club members looking for improvement. We don't question this course of action. We simply accept it as correct. Why? This is what we know; this is what the industry provides; this is what's available to us!

In golf, you've been conditioned to seek out teachers, not coaches, to help you with your game. Golf Magazine produces its list of Top 100 Teachers and Golf Digest publishes its list of America's 50

Greatest Teachers. The word "coach" doesn't seem to exist in golf—other than among college and high school teams. Just because the industry promotes a "teachers-giving-lessons" model, it doesn't make it right.

Now, don't get me wrong - the words "teachers" and "lessons" are not the problem. My daughter has trained as a dancer for years. She takes dance "lessons" from her dance "teacher." However, these lessons are quite different than those that we see in golf. My daughter attends dance lessons five hours per week. Her teacher continually reinforces and builds upon the skills that were learned in prior lessons. As my daughter masters certain skills, new higher level skills are introduced. Her practice of these skills is supervised, during which time her teacher provides on-going feedback and further instruction. As skills are developed, the teacher integrates them into a dance routine that is then trained to mastery so that it can be successfully performed at a later date in a recital, a play, or a competition. I refer to this process as "coaching." Call it what you may, the process is a proven, undeniable must to getting better at any skilled endeavor, whether it be dance or golf.

Think about it: Would you even know where to hire a golf coach if you decided you wanted one? Golf is taught by teachers, and teachers give lessons. From where I stand, and certainly looking through the lens of other sports, the golf teaching industry is broken. The industry provides lessons, and then sends an uninformed student off to a practice and playing environment void of all that is needed to continue learning. The solution to this broken system is two-fold: 1) teachers (I mean coaches!) must further their education and training so that they can offer and provide students with the coaching they deserve, and 2) students must seek out golf coaching, not just lessons, from a professional who is certified, qualified, and motivated to truly develop a player's golf skills. Without a change to the status quo, golfers will continue to struggle and to question, "Why am I not getting better?"

Summary

1. Hire a coach, not a lesson-giver. A coach will walk you through all the steps necessary to build your skills, not abandon you as soon as the lesson is over. Coaches provide on-going feedback and help facilitate the transfer of a skill onto the course. They teach you how to play the game, not just how to swing a golf club.
2. Recognize that there is a cost to getting better—advancing your education, improving your business outcomes, upgrading your computer system—all these improvements cost money. Take a detour away from the cheap route (i.e., books, magazines, self-teaching) and invest some time and money in coaching.
3. Suggest alternatives to the status quo. If you do have a teacher, ask him or her to become your coach. Suggest a different payment plan—possibly a monthly retainer for a defined number of hours of coaching. How about a bonus payment when your handicap reaches a certain level? Create a cost-effective arrangement within which you can spend more time with your coach (e.g., shorter, more frequent sessions, practicing in groups with friends).

Truth #7

FITNESS SETS THE CEILING FOR YOUR POTENTIAL

Golf is a recreational sport, much like tennis, biking, running and swimming. But for many years, it was linked more closely to bass fishing and ping pong than actual sport. The public's perception of golfers was that they rode in golf carts and smoked cigars, and thus anyone with a set of clubs, a sleeve of balls, and 4-5 hours of free time was fit to play 18 holes.

Gary Player and Arnold Palmer embraced the value of fitness long before it was widespread on the PGA Tour.

It's true that many years ago golfers did very little in the way of stretching or working out to get ready to play a round of golf. Most of the professional golfers on television in times past only perpetuated the myth that golfers weren't athletes. They looked more like Abbott and Costello than Mantle and Mays. There were a few players who challenged the norm, like Gary Player and Arnold Palmer, but for the most part, fitness did not seem to be an essential requirement for excelling at golf. In the 1980s, Greg Norman began to lay the foundation for a new athletic standard in golf. However, it wasn't until the early 2000s, when Tiger Woods and Annika Sorenstam convincingly dominated the game, that professional golfers started to be viewed as athletes. More and more Tour pros hit the gym to try and compete with Tiger and Annika, and it spawned a fitness revolution in golf that has forced many courses to expand—i.e., lengthening by hundreds of yards—in order to keep up with the game's longer hitters. Professional golfers on all tours are stronger, more flexible, and fitter than ever before.

"[Earlier in my career] there was no one in the gym. There was just me. . . . Now there are trainers that travel along with the Tour, trainers that travel with certain guys on the Tour. The guys have gotten bigger, stronger, more fit." –Tiger Woods

Beware of Teaching Malpractice

Unfortunately, the teaching industry has been a little late catching on to the growing fitness trend. Many teachers have little or no education in fitness as it pertains to golf, and while some are interested in expanding their knowledge to help their students, others are content to be paid an hourly fee standing on the lesson tee operating a video camera. Video certainly has its place in golf instruction, but when it is used to encourage students to move their bodies into swing positions that they are physically incapable of achieving, it borders on professional malpractice.

Many times, the reason why players can't achieve a certain ball-flight or position in their swings is because they have limited flexibility, poor strength, or even a prior injury that limits their range of motion. Yet, if teachers are unaware or untrained to assess such physical limitations, they will likely proceed with pulling out the video camera, drawing a few lines on a screen, and demonstrating that they don't know what they don't know.

Would a basketball coach teach you the mechanics of dunking a basketball if you couldn't jump high enough to reach the rim, or you had a bum ankle? Of course not, but we see it all the time in golf. The teacher will show your swing side-by-side next to Tiger's and say, "Notice how your left arm collapses in your backswing whereas Tiger maintains his extension. Also, note how Tiger has made a complete turn while maintaining his posture whereas you lose your spine angle at the top of your backswing." To try to have a student mimic Tiger's swing positions when he or she doesn't have Tiger's flexibility or strength is just wrong. Yet teachers use video models all of the time to support their ideal methodology, identify cause and effect, and persuade students to put their body and/or club into a different position.

If the underlying cause of poor swing technique is fitness, then a teacher should be knowledgeable enough to assess this and explain it to the student. The fix could then be to improve the student's fitness or even to develop a swing that accommodates the student's physical limitations. The bottom line is that if you want your swing to function like Tiger's, your body must function like his as well.

Although golf is not an aerobic sport like soccer or tennis, or an impact sport like football or hockey, it's still a physical sport which demands a certain level of physical competence (flexibility, strength, hand and arm speed, eye-hand coordination). If you have poor shoulder flexibility, how will you be able to consistently make a complete turn in your backswing? If your back begins to ache after practicing putts for only 10 minutes, how will you ever be able to put in the time required to build the new feel you want to have in your stroke?

Being physically unfit will not only limit how long you're able to practice, it will significantly increase your chances of getting injured. Golf is the one sport you can play well into your seventies and beyond, but only if you keep fit. The golf swing is not a natural motion; it places substantial and abnormal stress on the spine. To prevent injury, certainly as you get older, you must incorporate a fitness component into your golf training program.

If you've ever attended a Major League Baseball game, you've seen players warming up prior to the game, running sprints in the outfield or getting stretched out by trainers. They're not in the clubhouse having a drink or playing poker, like many golfers are. While golf is not as physical as most other sports, it's not chess, either. You have to get your body prepared for the rigors of playing

18 holes, just as you need to get it ready for a lesson or practice session. If you want to do the things that your coach is asking you to do (e.g., increase your backswing turn, maintain your posture), you have to be fit enough to do so.

Swing Errors are Often Caused by Physical Limitations

I'll frequently ask the golfers I see at PGA National what it is they're working on with their teacher. I remember one particular gentleman who said he'd been trying to eliminate an overly steep downswing for years, but always reverted back to this tendency under pressure. I said, "Well, what does your teacher think the cause of the problem is?" He replied, "He doesn't seem to know. He just keeps telling me to swing flatter and more around my body, but for some reason, I just can't seem to do it."

I asked him, "Have you ever talked with a fitness specialist to see if there might be a physical limitation that may be keeping you from doing what you want to do?" He said, "No," so we jumped in a cart and I drove him to the fitness center. I asked our Director of Fitness, Randy Myers, if he would take a look at this player from a fitness point of view.

Randy immediately began running the player through a series of fitness tests. Without any background knowledge of what the player was struggling with, Randy blurts out, "I bet you have a hard time staying on plane. How often have you been told that your swing is too steep?" I just laughed. Randy continued: "Because of the limited flexibility in your hip flexors and lats, you will have difficulty making a complete turn behind the ball and as a result just turn your shoulders. This often causes a player's swing to become too steep." Wow! The player was immediately relieved: "Thank goodness, I thought something was wrong with me, because I couldn't learn to do what my teacher kept asking me to do."

Your physical limitations can and will impact what you can and can't do with your golf swing. The chart below outlines several of golfers' most common complaints (effects) and the physical limitations (causes) that could be at the source of the problem. Knowing what you want your body to do is one thing, being able to physically do it is another. The stronger and more flexible you are, the more control you have over your muscles and the golf club. If you want to repeat your swing over and over and control your ball-flight—and who doesn't—then it helps to be in good physical condition.

COMMON PHYSICAL LIMITATIONS and RESULTING EFFECTS

Physical Limitation	Body Effect	Ball-Flight Effect
Poor shoulder flexibility →	*Arms collapse & reduce width in backswing* →	*Poor swing speed & loss of distance*
Poor abdominal strength & rotational flexibility →	*Lateral slide & inability to retain spine angle* →	*Slicing & lack of solid contact*
Poor gluteal (backside) strength →	*Poor lower body stability* →	*Poor swing speed & loss of distance*

Source: Randy Myers, Director of Fitness and the Tour Development Program at Sea Island Resorts

You won't see many professional golfers with poor fitness levels today. Many of them travel with their own personal trainers, and if they don't, they work with a certified trainer in the Tour fitness van or while they are home between tournaments.

There were no fitness trainers during Arnold Palmer's playing days, but that didn't stop him from becoming one of the most fit golfers of his era. But even "the King" had to learn from his mistakes. When Palmer first turned professional, he expected to pick up where he left off as an amateur and win right away, but he was surprised and disappointed when he didn't perform up to his expectation in his first professional event. "I expected so much more of myself," he said to me one day at Bay Hill Club & Lodge. I asked him, "Well, why do you think you weren't competitive?" He replied, "The other players were just better than I was." Palmer concluded that the reason they were better was because they must have out-practiced him and he vowed to make up the difference in the weeks to follow.

Palmer's next event wasn't for another several weeks, so he hit balls from sun up to sun down each day, determined to outwork his competition and defeat them the next time out. But in his first round back in competition, he played poorly once again. As it turns out, his hands were so blistered and sore from hitting balls that it was painful to just grip his clubs. The very next day, Palmer played even worse. He explained to me that, "because of how much I'd been practicing, my back started to spasm in the middle of my backswing and I had to do all I could to find the ball on the downswing." Needless to say, his finish was another disappointment.

I asked Mr. Palmer, "What did you learn from that experience?" He said, "I learned that I wasn't in shape, that my body couldn't support the work that I needed to put in. I realized that not only did the other players out-practice me, but they must have been in better shape as well to have put in that level of work." From that moment on, Palmer committed himself to being a well-conditioned player. He realized that fitness mattered.

All of the great players come to this realization at one point or another during their careers. Is it any surprise that the most dominant players have also been the most fit (Arnold Palmer, Tiger Woods, Annika Sorenstam)? Vijay Singh, known as "The Big Fijian," embraced fitness as a means to stay competitive with the younger talent qualifying for the PGA Tour each year. Singh won his first major (the 1998 PGA Championship) when he was 35, and he became the world's No. 1-ranked player at the age of 41. That year (2004), Singh won a career-high nine times, proof that if you maintain a healthy lifestyle and high degree of fitness, you can play this game well for a long time.

Summary

1. Stop pretending that golf isn't a physical sport. While it's certainly not rugby, it's not chess either.
2. If you think that ball-control errors might be caused by a physical limitation, and your coach acknowledges that he or she is not trained to assess this, ask your coach to refer you to a trained fitness specialist.
3. If you don't currently have a coach, seek out a golf coach who has been trained in fitness and understands how important strength, flexibility, and endurance are to your golf game. Each year, more and more golf coaches are pursuing golf fitness training and certification.
4. To ensure that you are prepared for the physical demands of the game, take the time to stretch before, during, and following each round that you play.

Truth #8

TO TRANSFER IT TO THE COURSE, PRACTICE LIKE YOU PLAY

Most golfers assume that if they practice a skill on the range, they will get better. They equate work (time spent on their game) with improvement. If their teacher gives them a drill or two to work on, and they spend 60 minutes on the practice range trying to master it on Friday, they expect that skill to magically appear on the golf course come Sunday. Some players even wait until the 30 minutes prior to their tee time to "cram for the test," and then they are disappointed when the work doesn't pay off once they are on the golf course.

No other sport is taught, learned, or practiced like golf. It's the only one I know that teaches the mechanics of a motion on the practice range and then expects the mechanics of that motion to naturally transfer to the golf course. There's practically no time spent scrimmaging or learning how to transfer a skill to the golf course. It's just not the way the game has traditionally been taught. Teachers teach on the lesson tee, and golfers learn the game on the practice range.

Think about the average 60-minute lesson today: For the first 10 to 15 minutes, the teacher observes and films you hitting balls; then you spend another 15 minutes looking at a video monitor while the teacher analyzes your swing motion and compares it to a model of Tiger Woods' swing; then you spend the next 15 to 20 minutes working on a few drills that will improve your fundamentals and swing technique; finally, you finish up with the teacher assigning you the homework that you should practice once you leave. Not one of these 60 minutes is spent on the course or working under conditions similar to those that exist on the course where your skills will ultimately be put to the test. I'm not saying every teacher organizes a lesson this way, but many of them do. That's how they were taught, and when they have eight or nine additional lessons to give on a particular day, there often isn't time to do much else.

Other Sports are Learned on the Field of Play, Why Not Golf?

Sports, other than golf, are learned on the field of play and under the conditions in which they are to be performed. Athletes learn skills in the context of how they will be utilized, and not in a sterile, perfect environment (i.e., on the lesson tee or practice range).

For example, if you played high school basketball, you spent much of your practice time on the court scrimmaging, going five-on-five, or running three-on-two fast break drills. Occasionally you went off with the other forwards to work on rebounding techniques or the other guards to develop better ball-handling skills, but you almost always practiced against another body in the court of play, just as you would in a "live" game. What's more, when the team lined up to shoot free throws at the end of practice, the coach added an element of pressure by forcing you or one of your teammates to make a free throw, threatening the team with "suicide" sprints should anybody miss the shot. Coaches did their best to simulate the kind of pressure and conditions you'd see in a game situation.

Some teams in the National Football League will pipe in crowd noise to their practice facility to simulate the conditions the squad will face in the opposing team's stadium. The coaches will have the quarterback bark out plays while the noise is turned up a notch, because what's the sense in practicing in conditions (absolute quiet) that will in no way simulate what they'll confront on Sunday?

You've heard the stories about Tiger Woods' dad, Earl Woods, and how he used to shake keys or roll a ball in front of Tiger while he was in the middle of his backswing. Earl did these things, not because he was mean-spirited, but because he wanted to create a learning environment that wasn't so sterile. The environment (course conditions, hazards, pressure,

Tiger Woods' extraordinary ability to scramble for par is a result of his practicing like he plays.

weather, fans) matters when it comes to learning, and Earl Woods understood that for his son to flourish in such situations, Tiger had to be exposed to them.

"As a kid, I might have been psycho, I guess, but I used to throw golf balls in the trees and try and somehow make par from them. I thought that was fun." –Tiger Woods

If you want the skill you're attempting to learn to show up on the course, you have to expose it, during training, to a range of on-course situations, from bare and fluffy lies to sidehill lies to in-between yardages. You have to be able to perform the skill consistently under pressure, as if you were playing in the final pairing of your club championship.

When I work with players on their chipping, I'll often have them hit chips from a variety of different lies (e.g., bare, fluffy, nestled down in the grass) to several different hole locations, not hit 20 consecutive chips from the same lie to the same hole. My adding variability to players' practice routines forces them to make the same type of decisions in practice that they will be confronted with on the course. They have to calculate how much resistance the club will encounter from the grass, where they have to land the ball, how the ball will check when it hits the green, and how far the ball will release—and they have to execute this process all over again on each consecutive ball. Since they don't hit two consecutive chips from the same lie to the same target, they can't get lazy and simply repeat the motion that they made on the previous shot. They are practicing like they play.

Most golfers head to the short-game practice area with a technical tip and a bucket of balls. They then hit every ball to the same hole from the same lie. Not surprisingly, they often get in a groove and start experiencing a lot of success. They start to think, "Aha, I've got it." But that's because the conditions are sterile, unchanging, predictable, and familiar. What happens when they get on the golf course come Sunday and the ball is nestled up against the first collar of rough? They chunk the ball three feet! Worse yet, they can't understand why they fatted the shot when they hit 50 successful chips in practice a few days earlier. The assumption is that the cause is "mental," that they "choked," when in reality, the skill has not yet been mastered; it hasn't yet progressed through the transfer step.

Simulate On-Course Conditions in Practice

The biggest excuse I hear as to why golf is not learned in the field of play, like other sports, is because the courses are generally not available for practice. But not all practice has to be conducted on the course in order for the skill to be transferred. The important thing is that you practice in conditions similar to those within which you play. If you take the chipping example above and introduce different variables by changing your lies and targets, then you are forced to make decisions and vary your strategy on each and every shot. That's simulation training.

Zach Johnson may have got a practice round or two in at Augusta National prior to his title run at the 2007 Masters. But that didn't mean he couldn't practice the shots he was going to face at Augusta beforehand. Feeling Zach needed to perform exceptionally well in his wedge game to contend at the Masters, his coach, Mike Bender, built him a wedge course at his practice facility at Timacuan Golf Club in Lake Mary, Florida. The course featured eight concrete plates as targets, each built into an upslope so they were easily seen—and heard. The first plate was set at 30 yards, and the remaining plates staggered in 10-yard increments up to 100 yards. To complete the course, Zach had to hit all eight plates.

Scrimmaging every day for weeks on the wedge course, Johnson was able to sharpen his wedge game—and, in particular, his distance control—to the point where it would be the difference-maker at Augusta. Of the 16 par-5s he played that week, he laid up on all of them and made birdie 11 times with his wedges. While Johnson didn't have the length to compete with the likes of Tiger Woods and Phil Mickelson at Augusta, he had the wedge game to beat them, thanks to the simulation training he completed at Timacuan.

Pressure is another important condition that needs to be present during practice in order for your skill to successfully transfer to the golf course. Fortunately, pressure can be simulated fairly easily in practice. How? Set a goal and establish a consequence for success or failure. Furthermore, make sure that the consequence is significant—rewards for success should be highly valued and penalties for failure should be equally painful.

The Tour pros with whom I work are highly motivated by money. It's not that they need the money, they just like taking it from me, and they hate giving it up—it's a pride thing! So, while training, we make a lot of bets. We establish a mutually agreed upon practice goal and then apply money as the reward/consequence.

Here's one putting game I have my pros play regularly: I ask them to play 18 "holes" on the practice putting green, each one of them a par 2, and their goal is to play all 18 holes in even par or better—in essence, two-putting from 18 different locations around the green. However, there are rules they have to follow:

1. All putts are from outside of 10 feet. For putts inside 20 feet, they cannot leave the ball short of the hole, nor can they hit it more than two feet past the hole. If they do, they're penalized a stroke. (Example: If a player leaves the first putt short of the hole but makes the next putt, the player cards a bogey 3, because of being penalized one shot for a ball outside of the error zone. If the player one-putts, the player cards a birdie.)
2. For putts more than 20 feet but inside 30 feet, the error zone is extended to three feet past the hole. Again, if the player misses long or short of the error zone he or she is penalized a stroke.
3. On putts more than 30 feet but less than 40, the error zone is extended to four feet (three feet of error past the hole and one foot in front).
4. On putts from 41 to 50 feet, the error zone becomes five feet, with three feet in back of the hole and two feet in front.

Players select and play 18 random holes around the putting green (six holes between 10-20 feet, six holes between 21-30 feet, and six holes between 31-50 feet). As they play, the strokes can add up quickly if their distance control is not very good. For Tour players, the goal we establish for this game is "even par for 18 holes." Additionally, we add a consequence by placing a bet of a defined dollar value for every stroke that they are either over or under par. If they are over par, they pay me, if under par, I pay them.

This simulation training game separates the good putters from the bad in a hurry. It places players in a practice situation in which score matters, they have to read each putt, and they have to control the speed of the putt or they incur a penalty. Also, pressure is introduced via a goal and a bet.

If you find that you have difficulty taking your game from the practice range to the golf course, take a closer look at how you are practicing. If you can't practice on the golf course, then at a minimum, practice like you play.

Summary

1. Whenever possible, take your training to the course. Recognize that skills have to progress through the transfer step to be mastered and what better place to do this then on the course. Ask your coach for playing lessons designed specifically to transfer the skills you've been developing on the range and practice greens.
2. Work with your coach to create practice games, drills, and conditions which simulate the conditions you face on the golf course.
3. When practicing on the range or in a short-game area, vary your targets and lies. Don't always hit the same shot to the same target. For example: On the range, try hitting one shot to the left half of a green, then the next shot to the right half, then one to the front half, and then one to the back half of the green. By varying your targets and the distance demands of your shots, you are increasing the likelihood of your skill transferring to the course.
4. Integrate mental demands (e.g., distractions, pressure, decision-making) into your skill practice sessions. To facilitate the transfer of your skills, spend more time practicing in challenging, simulated on-course conditions.

Truth #9

THE WEAKEST LINK BREAKS UNDER PRESSURE

People assume that when something breaks down on the golf course, it's due to a mental error. If their Saturday foursome comes down to the last hole and they miss a 5-footer to win or extend the match, it's not because they're a bad putter, it's because they "choked." Rather than recognize that they tend to miss a lot of short putts under pressure, they go on assuming that their putting stroke is fine and chalk it up to another case of the nerves.

I see it all the time when I do skills assessments with players. They think their problem is mental, but when I run their skills through a variety of tests it turns out the reason why they three-putt is they lack speed control from 30 feet and beyond. Remember the PGA Tour player I discussed in the Introduction who thought the reason he was missing cuts was because he was doing something wrong mentally? When his skills were put to the test on the range, he couldn't hit five out of 10 balls on the green from 160 yards out. A Tour-level player! It never even crossed his mind that the cause of his error was his lack of practice, and thus the decline of his skill; he was sure it was mental.

Pressure Will Expose Your Weakness

On the golf course, the skill that breaks down under pressure is more often than not the one that is the weakest part of your game. If you have a tendency under pressure to chunk your chip shots from just off the green, but you have no trouble hitting the fairway with your driver, it's not that you are "mental" with your chipping, it's more likely that chipping is a weakness in your game.

Think about your golf skills as links in a metal chain. One link represents your putting, another link your chipping, another your driving, and so on. Now imagine attaching one end of the chain to the ceiling and allowing the chain to hang freely. Now, if one of the links of the chain were flawed or poorly constructed, the chain could still hang freely from the ceiling. However, if you reached up and tugged on the chain a few times, it could possibly give way—and if it did, where do you think the chain would break? At the weakest link—of course!

Pressure will pull on your chain of golf skills.

When you're in the comfort zone of the practice range (and your chain of skills is hanging freely), the flaws in your game are not so apparent. However, when you place your game under pressure (and tug on your chain of skills), suddenly your weak link is exposed and likely to be the skill that breaks down.

The reason golf is so challenging is that on the course during competition, there are many conditions that "tug on your chain" - a bet with a friend, a three-foot putt to tie the match, a stiff wind, a water hazard, deep fescue rough. It could be anything that taxes you mentally during a round. As your skills are "tugged upon" you will find that certain ones are vulnerable—you'll hit a drive or two out of play, chunk a wedge shot, or possibly 3-putt several greens. When this happens, you hear players say they "choked," but what's actually happening is that their weakest link is showing itself, usually at the most inopportune moment. Rather than get upset and label yourself a "choker," take note of what skill is breaking down. Inform your coach of your findings and start the process of repairing your weakest link. As you firm up that skill through training, the skill will be much more reliable under pressure in future rounds.

"Golf is like a chain. You always have to work on the weakest links." –George Archer

A common weak link among high-handicap golfers is the three-foot putt. If you are a high handicapper, you never have to putt these out. Anything within three or four feet of the hole is considered a "gimme" among friends. Part of this is done for speed of play reasons, and also to spare the potential embarrassment of missing one. Thus, it's a rare instance when you have to make a putt from this distance. However, in competition or where there's money on the line, that gimme becomes a must make. It's not surprising that these putts are commonly missed, leading to the conclusion, "I choked." It isn't that you choked, it's that you never mastered the skill under competition because your friends kept giving you the putts. The solution becomes all too apparent—work on your three-footers, and stop accepting all of those gimmes!

Explaining Golf's Famous Collapses

There have been several notable "collapses" in majors over the years—Greg Norman at the 1996 Masters; Jean Van de Velde at the 1999 Open Championship; Phil Mickelson at the 2006 U.S. Open; Kenny Perry at the 2009 Masters. But not all of these failures were "chokes," as they've come to be known. In fact, I'd argue that most of them were the result of the player's weakest link breaking down under pressure.

Take a look at Phil Mickelson, who had come agonizingly close to winning the U.S. Open on several occasions prior to 2006. At Winged Foot, the man known as Lefty nursed a one-shot lead heading into the 72nd and final hole—a 450-yard par 4. Trying to hit his bread-and-butter "baby slice"—which had been so effective for him at the Masters a few months earlier—Mickelson over-cut his drive and hit it way left behind some trees. He then tried to force his next shot trough a small opening in the trees and again cut it too much, this time hitting a tree. Mickelson wound up making a double bogey—his only double bogey of the tournament—and missing a playoff by one shot, afterwards uttering one of the most famous lines in major championship history, "I am such an idiot."

Mickelson's decision to hit driver off the tee and then to try a risky second shot instead of pitching out drew a lot of criticism, and had media and fans all believing it was just another classic Mickelson "choke job." But a look at Lefty's driving stats for the week and the year suggested something different, that it was a case of his weakest link unable to handle the pressure of the moment. For the week, Mickelson hit less than 50 percent of his fairways, and for the year he ranked among the worst (160th) on the PGA Tour in driving accuracy at 58.61 percent. Even he admitted as much in the painful press conference afterwards, saying, "I just couldn't hit a fairway all day."

Although some assigned blame to Mickelson's decision-making on 18, ultimately, it was his weakest link that dragged him down under pressure.

Van de Velde's collapse at Carnoustie in 1999 could be chalked up to poor decision-making. Holding a commanding three-shot lead heading into the final hole, he could have wedged his way to a double bogey and won. But he chose driver off of the tee, and while his tee shot stayed dry, it finished well right of the burn, setting up a comedy of errors that followed and led to a triple bogey 7. Decision-making is without a doubt an essential skill in golf, and for Van de Velde, it appears to have been the skill that was susceptible to the pressure of the moment.

Norman's unfortunate fall at the Masters in 1996—he led Nick Faldo by six shots heading into the final round and lost by five—would best be described as "one of those days" where seemingly everything that could go wrong, did. Norman, who shot a course-record tying 63 in the first round at Augusta National, still led Faldo by three shots heading into the par-4 9th hole, but then went bogey-bogey-bogey-double bogey to trail by two. He wound up shooting a 78.

Greg Norman's epic collapse at the 1996 Masters had a lot to do with his weakest link breaking under pressure.

It would be hard to pin-point one thing that went wrong with Norman's game on that Sunday afternoon in Georgia, but the two shots that cost Norman most were the iron shots he hit on hole Nos. 12 and 16, both par 3s. Each one found the water and resulted in a double bogey, costing Norman four vital strokes. A look at his season stats for that year found that Norman ranked just 149th on the PGA Tour in greens hit in regulation (63.6 percent)—a weak link for sure.

The then-48-year-old Kenny Perry held a two-shot lead with two holes to play at the 2009 Masters, after nearly making a hole-in-one on the same par-3 16th hole that doomed Norman. It looked like the native of Kentucky was on his way to getting fitted for a green jacket when the wheels suddenly came ajar. He made bogey on No. 17 after blading an 8-iron chip across the green. The collapse was completed on the second playoff hole—the par-4 10th—when he hit his approach shot well left of the green and again made bogey.

Clearly the shot that cost him most was the chip on 17. Had he made par there, he would've taken a two-shot cushion into No. 18. Following his loss, a devastated Perry clued the world in on his chipping struggles. It turns out he skulled two similar chips on the 15th and 18th holes in the final round of the 2008 John Deere Classic, also forcing a playoff (an event he won, however). "I can't stop my right hand," confessed Perry. "When I get a little nervous, it wants to shoot a little bit and I can't calm it down." Perry recognized that under pressure his weakest link, his chipping, was prone to break down.

In that same Masters, Mickelson made a furious charge on Sunday with a 6-under-par 30 on the front nine, closing to within one shot of the lead. Even after finding Rae's Creek with his tee shot on the par-3 12th, Mickelson had a chance to grab a share of the lead with a 4-foot eagle putt on the par-5 15th. His putt missed the hole entirely. On the next hole he had another fairly short putt of five feet for birdie and he missed again. Mickelson shot 1 over on the back and finished three shots out of a playoff.

Afterwards, the "choke" label was being loosely thrown around Mickelson again. But a look at his stats for 2009 showed a propensity to miss short putts: He ranked 154th on Tour in putts inside five feet (95.32 percent). Figure in the severity of the slopes at Augusta National and the green speeds, and it's understandable that this weak link would succumb to such extreme pressure.

Summary

1. Stop calling yourself a "choker." Don't assume that competitive errors are due to a lack of mental toughness. The average recreational golfer under the pressure of a club championship environment is going to experience a breakdown in skills. Take note of which skills succumb to the pressure, and then go improve those skills.
2. If you've just started working on a new skill, give yourself a break. Assume that under pressure it may break down because you haven't yet had the time to master it. Instead, look at pressure situations as an opportunity to expose the skill to transfer conditions, thus training it even further.
3. Once you've started to experience success with a particular skill under comfortable conditions, begin exposing it to increasing levels of pressure (e.g., windy conditions, more difficult golf courses, challenging playing partners, money matches). Initially, the skill may break down under pressure, however, over time you should begin to see the skill becoming more reliable—you are on the road to mastery.

Truth #10

UNDER COMPETITION, YOUR BRAIN REVERTS TO THE FAMILIAR

How many times have you said to yourself, "If I could only put it together for all 18 holes?" You're cruising along through six, seven holes, playing some of the best golf you've played in months, when suddenly your old snap-hook or pull-slice reappears. Or those putts that were tracking on line and finding the bottom of the hole are suddenly veering to the left and missing the cup entirely.

It happens with almost all of us mere mortals. We have stretches of three, six, nine holes where we play up to the maximum of our abilities—when we begin to think we've got a special round going—and then we run smack into a tornado of bad shots and come crashing back down to earth. As soon as the pressure begins to intensify, our old tendency to hook or slice the ball rears its ugly head.

As we discussed in Truth #9, your weakest skill breaks down under pressure. The question becomes, breaks down to what? More often than not, under competition, your skill reverts to the familiar. What I mean by "to the familiar" is to your most common prior ball-flight.

Under competition, your brain will revert back to what it knows best, and if you haven't developed or trained a new skill long enough, the old pattern will show up. If your tendency under pressure is to swing out-to-in with an open clubface and lose your shots off to the right, and you've spent all but a few lessons trying to get rid of that slice, guess what? You're likely to see the return of your slice as you are staring at a long forced carry or a tight driving hole with out-of-bounds to the right. When the pressure is on, it's very difficult to consciously control your physical movements—your mental resources are a bit consumed trying to manage the emotional and attention demands of the situation.

Quick Fixes are Short-Lived

At many corporate or charity golf events, the organizers will pay a teaching pro to provide a brief clinic or to walk up and down the driving range as players warm up, offering them help with their swings. The majority of these players slice the golf ball, but after spending a few minutes with the teacher, they may hit a few straight shots and even an occasional draw (experienced teachers have quick fixes that they can apply in the short term to band-aid a slice). However, as soon as these players get under the gun on the course, their familiar slice returns. Often you'll hear them exclaim, "Gosh, I was hitting the ball so well when I was with the pro. What happened?"

This same experience occurs among seasoned players at local golf clubs all the time. Players take a lesson during the week from their teacher, hit a few buckets of balls over the next few days, experience success during these practice sessions, and show up for their regular foursome match on the weekend fully expecting to reap the benefit of that week's lesson. The swing thought they received from their teacher may even work for a few holes; however, eventually the conditions get tough, a hazard looms, or someone presses the bet, and the old habit resurfaces. At that point, they figure, "Oh well, that tip I got from my pro must not have been that good," and they abandon it forever.

The fact is, there may have been nothing wrong with the pro's recommendation; there just wasn't enough time to learn it, to own it. Until you've fully stored the new program in your brain, it's unlikely that it will show up consistently under pressure. The more repetition and transfer conditions you walk the skill through, the more ingrained the skill becomes in your body. Until you truly learn the new skill, when the going gets tough, you're going to revert back to what your brain knows best (i.e., the familiar).

Let's say you're an avid runner with many 10Ks and marathons under your belt, and one day you read a story about a trainer who's had tremendous success improving people's times by teaching them how to run backwards. He's discovered that running backwards is a more efficient way of running and stresses the body less. Intrigued, you attend his five-day school and, sure enough, at the end of the week you're running backwards with tremendous form for miles through the park, hardly breaking a sweat.

Two weeks later you and your family take a long-awaited trip out to Yellowstone National Park. You're hiking through the woods when suddenly you encounter a large grizzly bear about 10 yards in front of you on the trail. The bear looks your way, and out of anxiety, you instinctively start to run. Are you going to run backwards? Of course you're not! You're going to turn around, face forwards, and run for your life. Why? Because it's the most familiar way you know to run. You've been running forwards for your entire life, and a five-day "running backwards" school isn't sufficient to re-program your brain to run in an entirely new fashion, especially when a grizzly bear may be chasing you.

This regression to the familiar is what tends to happen on the golf course as well. It might not be as dramatic or life-threatening, but under pressure, your brain is going to latch onto the most efficient motor program it has to use. If you've been consistently slicing the ball—coming over the top with an open clubface—for 20 years, don't expect that habit to just disappear because your teacher showed you how to draw the ball in your last lesson. You may have hit a few good draws on the range with the clubhead releasing properly on plane. That doesn't mean that your steep, out-to-in swing path won't reappear on the 18th tee come Sunday when you're playing with your buddies for money. In all likelihood, it will.

Dance with the Partner You Know

Now, here's what most recreational golfers don't know: A slice isn't necessarily a bad thing. Not if it's a predictable, playable error. As long as you don't waste your entire round trying to fix your slice, you can make the most of a less than perfect ball-flight. There comes a time when you simply have to put your skill development on hold and dance with the partner you know (i.e., play with what you have).

> "I have always felt you have to play golf by feel. All athletes, when they get in pressure situations, revert to what they know." – Jack Nicklaus

If your ball-flight naturally curves from left to right, especially under pressure, then aim more left to allow the ball to fade toward the center of the fairway or green. That's what a PGA Tour player would do. He wouldn't stop in the middle of a tournament to try and fix a ball-flight pattern just because it wasn't perfect. If the ball-flight was repeatable and predictable, he'd play it.

During competition, great athletes like Hall of Fame pitcher Jim Palmer play with what they know.

I recall a conversation that I had with Hall of Fame pitcher Jim Palmer, who played his entire career for the Baltimore Orioles. I asked him, "Where would you focus your attention while throwing a curve ball?" He immediately responded, "It would depend on how much the ball was curving at that time. Normally, I would focus on starting the ball at a right-handed batter's left shoulder and allow it to curve into the catcher's mitt. But on some days the ball would be curving quite a bit, so I would focus on a point behind the batter's back, and then trust that the ball would curve even more." Jim Palmer would play with the ball curvature that showed up on any given day, and not waste time trying to change it.

If you haven't had the time to practice and master a new ball-flight, play your familiar, more predicable shot pattern when competing. You can certainly allocate some playing time on the golf course to work on transferring new skills to the course, but when your score matters, it's all about putting the ball in the hole in the least amount of strokes. How many times have you seen Tiger Woods or some other PGA Tour pro come out with their "C" game and still manage to post a number in the 60s? It happens all of the time. Why? Because the pros are adept at dancing with the partner they know, playing for their predictable errors, missing shots in the right places and avoiding big numbers. They know how to make par even when they don't have their "A" game. Tiger Woods' return to golf at the 2010 Masters (his first event following a turbulent five-month layoff) was a perfect example. On the final Sunday, the rust started to show as Woods struggled with his swing, hitting a variety of pull hooks, blocks, and pop-ups off the tee. Yet he still managed to make two eagles and shot a 69.

Tiger is a master at playing with what he has on any given day. In an appearance with former swing coach Butch Harmon on Golf Channel's "Academy Live" in 2000, Woods discussed how he relies on his go-to shot—a shot that, although not ideal for the situation, is predictable and reliable under competition when he is not comfortable with his game.

"Trying to get the ball in the hole in as few strokes as possible when you are not playing well, that's a task," said Woods. "One of the things I've found that works best for me is to [have] a go-to shot. At Firestone (the 1999 WGC-NEC Invitational), I was putting the ball back in my stance and punching a lot of shots. That's one of the shots I've learned to try and get me in the clubhouse. I put [the ball] back in my stance, [make] a little shorter backswing, shorter follow-through. One of the things Butch has taught me is the less the ball stays in the air, the less time it has to go off-line."

Top Gun Navy pilots are trained how to fly fighter jets, not fix them. While engaged in aerial combat, these pilots do not cease fighting and fix their jets because they are dissatisfied with the way they are maneuvering through the air. In combat, it's all about decision-making, self-management, and flying the jet.

You should look at your golf swing as your fighter jet: Once you get to the course, it's time to fly with what you have. Don't spend the entire round trying to fix what's wrong with it or make it perform better. During competition, choose to be the pilot, not the mechanic.

Summary

1. Rather than blame your coach when your newly learned ball-flight doesn't initially hold up under competition, recognize that it's normal to revert to your more familiar ball-flight tendency for awhile. Until you've put in the time to master the new ball-flight, it's not going to be too reliable under pressure.
2. When score really matters, play your most familiar ball-flight. If you slice the ball, aim farther left so the ball can fade back to the center of the fairway. Don't spend the entire round attempting to fix your slice.
3. Develop a go-to shot for competition—one that you're familiar with and you can repeat under pressure. Take some time in practice to identify and to master your pressure proof go-to shot.
4. Ask your coach for playing lessons during which he or she shows you how to play the course using your most familiar ball-flight and expected errors. Don't spend the lesson working on your swing mechanics on the course; instead, learn to play the course with what you've got.

Truth #11

YOU WILL PLAY AVERAGE OR BETTER ONLY 50 PERCENT OF THE TIME

People often have unrealistic expectations of how they will play when they step onto the golf course. They expect to play up to their full potential, not to their average. If their goal is to break 80, they're not happy with an 82 even if it's better than their average score.

There are several reasons why people's expectations are out of line on the golf course. For one, players don't recognize all of the inconsistencies and variables that contribute to their score on any given day (e.g., weather, green conditions, luck). There are certain things in golf you can't control, and thus you have much less control of your 18-hole score than you think. The bounces aren't always going to go your way. For example, during the broadcast of the 2010 Masters, slow motion replay showed a twig fall from the sky directly into Phil Mickelson's line just as he was stroking a putt for birdie on the par-5 2nd hole. The twig knocked the ball off-line, causing Mickelson to miss the putt at a time when he was leading in the final round. Imagine how easily such a freak incident could affect a player's mindset if he or she did not accept those things are just not within his or her control.

Your final score on any given day is an accumulation of many factors. There will be days when your swing just doesn't feel right, the pins are tucked to the edges of the greens, the wind is howling, the greens are bumpy, the fairways aren't running out, or the bunkers are wet (i.e., the conditions won't be advantageous to scoring).

Secondly, how many times have you heard someone say something like, "I would've broken 80 had I not hit the ball in the water," or "Had I not three-putted four times on the back nine?" No kidding! There's only one problem—those shots did in fact happen. Making hypothetical mental subtractions following a round only perpetuates a player's unrealistic expectations of what he or she should shoot. A round of golf is a summation of your great, average, and poor shots combined. You can't eliminate the poor ones and then tell yourself that you are better than what you actually shot—the poor shots are part of the game, part of your skill, and thus part of your score.

Finally, players too often head to the first tee with what I refer to as "a case of the shoulds." They begin the round with a score in their mind of what they "should" shoot—their expected score—and more often than not, they don't live up to their expectation. The problem is, the score they expect to shoot is much lower than the score they are likely to shoot! Why? All too often, players use their Handicap Index to calculate their expected score—and in doing so, they set themselves up for failure right from the start.

Your Handicap Index Can Be Misleading

Players often misinterpret what their Handicap Index represents; they mistakenly think that if they're an 18-handicap they should shoot 90 (level-par 72 plus 18). In reality, they're much more likely to shoot 95. If you begin a round thinking that you "should" post a score that is five shots lower than what is most likely to occur, you've just set yourself up for disappointment.

A score of "72 plus your Handicap Index" more accurately reflects your scoring potential than it does your scoring average (the score you're more likely to shoot), because the USGA Handicap System eliminates your 10 worst scores and calculates your index from the 10 best (from your last 20 rounds). Your handicap reflects only your best days. A better predictor of your scoring average, and thus of your most likely score, would be the "median" of your last twenty rounds.

If you recall from your math studies, the median is that number in a group of numbers at which half the scores are above, and half the scores are below. If you were an 18-handicapper, it is likely that the median of your 20 posted scores would be 95, not 90 (72+18). A median score of 95 would suggest that you would have a 50 percent chance of shooting 95 or above, and a 50 percent chance of shooting 95 or below. More often than not, you're going to shoot something in the neighborhood of your median score. You should expect half of your rounds to come in at or above 95, and half at or below.

Let's look at the example of an actual club player—let's call him Ron—whose Handicap Index is 6.4. Here is a list of his last 20 scores that were used to calculate his handicap:[1]

78	84	77	82	80	86	85	86	83	81
82	77	80	84	82	75	78	83	82	85

Here's what the scores would look like charted along a normal bell curve:

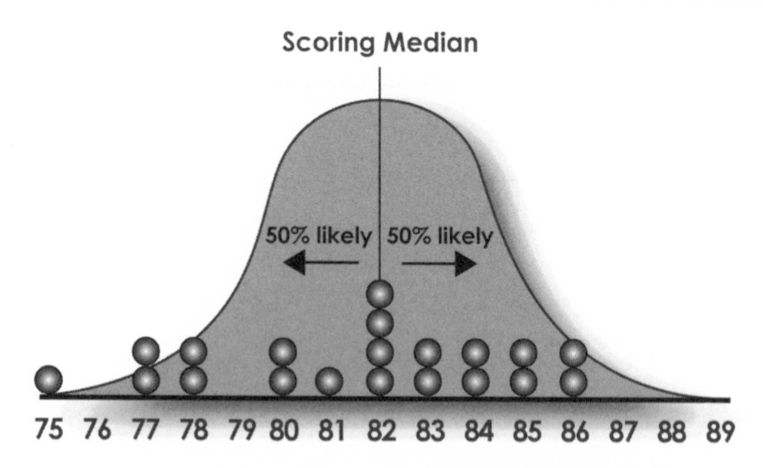

As you can see, Ron's median score is an 82—eight rounds fell above 82, eight rounds below 82, and four right at 82. The reality

1 Each score is based on Handicap Differential, which calculates a player's adjusted gross score considering the USGA Course Rating and Slope Rating of the course, and the average Slope Rating of a course of standard difficulty. If, for example, you posted a 95 from the blue tees at a very difficult course and a 95 from the blue tees at a much easier course, it's going to re-adjust the round from the more difficult course as a better score.

is that Ron is just as likely to shoot an 86 as he is to shoot a 78 (+ or - 4 shots of his median). For him to expect to shoot in the 70s because he has a 6.4 Handicap Index would be a mistake. As you can see from his bell curve, only five (25 percent) of Ron's scores are in the 70s.

Should Ron be upset or question why he failed on the day he posts an 84? Certainly not. As Ron's chart of scores indicate, a score of 84 would be well within his normal range of scores. Using his 6-handicap as a predictor of what Ron should shoot is a common mental miscalculation among golfers, leading them to approach their rounds with unrealistic expectations, and leave their rounds with unjustified disappointment.

The handicap system was not developed to help golfers set their expectation of what they "should" shoot. It was designed to build a fair and even playing system, so that a 20-handicapper could compete with a 5-handicapper and both have a fair chance of winning.

Inconsistency from One Day to Another is Normal and Expected

Anyone who has ever taken a statistics class has heard the phrase "regression toward the mean." What this principle suggests is that over time, you will play to your average. If you go out on Saturday and shoot 90, but your scoring average is 95, your odds of shooting 90 again on Sunday are actually the same odds of you shooting 100 (both scores are 5 shots from your scoring average). Yet, when players shoot 90 and 100 on two consecutive days, they are satisfied with day one, but start searching for something that they did wrong on day two. Obviously, they didn't play as well, but the only thing they did wrong on day two was to go into it with a scoring average of 95—thus, opening the door for the possibility of shooting 100. Were their scoring average to be 80, then a score of 100 becomes quite unlikely.

A look at Tiger Woods' results for 2009 shows that he played 66 rounds of golf on the PGA Tour with a scoring average of 68.84. Of his 66 rounds, Tiger shot 69 or above 36 times, and 68 or below 30 times, thus his scoring median was 69. More significantly, of those 66 rounds, all but four rounds fell between 64 and 74—a 10-shot differential.

A glance at the world's No. 2 player that year, Phil Mickelson, shows that he played a similar number of rounds as Woods in 2009—67. Of those 67 rounds, Mickelson shot 71 or above 34 times, and 70 or below 33 times. Lefty's scoring average for the season was 70.22, his scoring median was 71, and all but eight of his scores fell between a 65 and a 75.

What these numbers show is that even the best players in the world shoot equal to or better than their median score only 50 percent of the time. The flipside of this finding is that golfers play equal to or below their median score 50 percent of the time as well. Furthermore, the variability in Tiger and Phil's scores suggests that the search for consistency embarked upon by most amateurs is a losing proposition. Even on the PGA Tour, scores fluctuate within a 10-shot range (plus or minus five strokes of a player's median score).

Inconsistency is normal and expected—yet players continue to feel defeat when they experience it.

What is so special about players of the caliber of Woods and Mickelson is not their consistency, it's that their scoring median is so low. As you can see on the chart below, when you chart Tiger and Phil's distribution alongside the distribution of our single digit handicapper, Ron, it becomes all too evident what would happen were they to compete in the same arena. Ron has a similar dispersion of scores around his scoring median with one very significant difference—his median score is about 12 shots higher. Even if Ron played to the best of his capabilities, he wouldn't beat Tiger or Phil on their worst day!

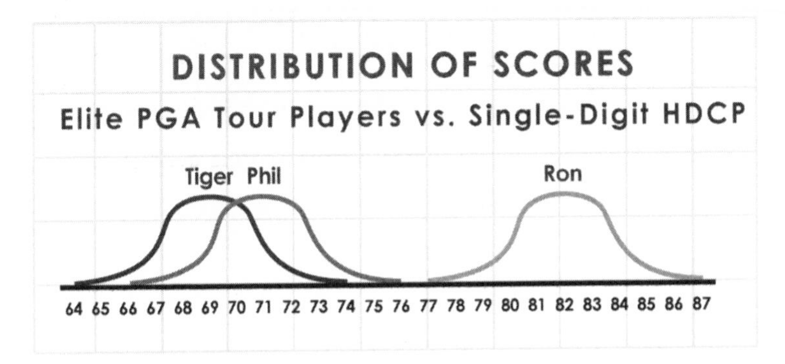

The other image that you might note above is that Tiger and Phil's distributions overlap, suggesting that on any given day either player could beat the other. True! However, over the course of a season, a two-shot difference in scoring median is significant—this gap resulted in Tiger winning $5 million more than Phil in 2009.

The longer you play, the better chance the better player has of winning." –Jack Nicklaus

Jack Nicklaus once said, "During my prime, I never really felt pressure because I always thought that my worst game was better than the next best player's best game." Top players understand that they play at or above their average only 50 percent of the time, so they spend the bulk of their energy training to shift their entire bell curve of scores as far from their competition's bell curve as possible.

Jack Nicklaus didn't always need his "A" game to beat his competitors.

Summary

1. Stop trying to explain away your poor scores—the fact is that you are going to play at or below your average 50 percent of the time. Accept this, but don't accept that your average has to remain the same. You can get better.
2. Recognize that the scores you post will naturally fluctuate around your median score. This expected inconsistency (within plus or minus five of your median score) is normal. Rather than striving to be more "consistent," strive to lower your median score by pursuing coaching and walking your skills through all four steps in the learning process (see Truth #3).
3. Stop using your Handicap Index as a means to set your expectation of what you should shoot. Better yet, play each round without a scoring expectation—simply give your best effort on each and every shot.
4. Accept that there are many factors in golf that are outside of your control, yet affect your day-to-day scores (weather, green conditions, luck). Control what you can (your decisions, your training, your preparation) and let those unfortunate, uncontrollable factors roll off of your back.

Truth #12

GOLF IS A GAME OF MISSES

Most golfers not only have unrealistic expectations about what they should shoot, but they think they ought to hit every shot dead-solid perfect. If they miss their target by 10 or 20 yards, they get very upset and start playing the blame game. They fault everything from their swing to their aim to a flock of birds passing over their head in the middle of their backswing. They never leave any margin for error, which is why they so often find themselves in impossible predicaments, scrambling to make bogey or worse.

There's a reason amateurs miss their approach shots short of the green, and it's not because they have a hard time getting an exact yardage. No, it's because they assume they will hit the ball to the best of their ability, and they rarely take into account all of the variables that can impact the distance of the shot—hitting the ball off-center, the wind, the temperature, the lie of the ball, the green's elevation, the pressure of the situation, etc. Again, they only think about the perfect shot, not the average distance they hit a particular club most of the time.

Plan for Your Misses

The game's best players are smart enough to realize that they can't control where every shot goes. They can be pretty accurate—to within a few yards with their wedges—but they know where to bail out if they have to, and what side of the green (short, long, left, right) to favor should they not hit the ball precisely where they want to.

"Always consider where you might end up if you hit a less than perfect shot." –Annika Sorenstam

As they run through their pre-shot checklist with their caddie, Tour players factor in a number of things: the yardage to the front of the green and the flagstick; the distance between the flag and a particular bunker, a false front, or a water hazard they're trying to avoid; the firmness of the green; how much the wind will affect the carry and release of the ball. Eventually, they come up with an exact yardage and position on the green where they want to land the ball—one that factors in what could happen if they miss their intended target. They aim to accommodate their miss.

Because Tour players plan for a miss, they rarely find themselves in a position from which they can't make par. If a pin is tucked right on a green with a water hazard just to the right of the green, Tour players aim more toward the left-center of the green so that if they do miss their shot some, they will not end up in the water. Tour pros hit what I refer to as "aggressively smart" shots. They select a smart target, one that considers where a miss will still be playable, and then they aggressively focus their attention on hitting their smart target. They do not want their mind to get lazy and drift away from their smart target to a more risky target that, were they to miss it, would lead to a sure bogey.

Amateurs, on the other hand, are not as disciplined. They too often plan for their ideal shot, and when they don't hit it, they question what went wrong with their swing. They mistakenly expect that they are going to hit the ball perfectly and they make the mistake of planning for it as they select their intended target. Amateurs often fire at tucked pins on greens, attempt carries over water from difficult lies, try to cut the corner of a dogleg, and go for that miracle recovery shot from the trees when punching out would be the smart play. All fine when they pull it off, but when they miss, they make double or triple bogey, at best.

Golf legend Bobby Jones pointed out that "Golf is said to be a humbling game, but it is surprising how many people are either not aware of their weaknesses or else reckless of consequences." Given all of the variables present during a round of golf and the difficulty of hitting a little white ball flush in the sweet spot of the clubface, even players of Jones' caliber cannot predict with much confidence exactly where their ball is going to end up. So what do they do? They consider the potential consequences and then plan for and play within their "range of error."

Phil Mickelson is known as one of the most aggressive players the game has ever seen. One needn't look any further than the second shot he produced on the par-5 13th hole at the 2010 Masters. Leading by one shot, Mickelson pulled his tee shot to the right into the woods at Augusta National Golf Club. Staring at a four-foot wide gap between two trees and 207 yards to the flagstick, Mickelson took a mighty rip with a 6-iron off the pine straw and miraculously hit the ball to four feet. Had his ball landed just a yard or two shorter it would've tumbled into Rae's Creek, and we certainly wouldn't be talking about one of golf's greatest shots ever.

In the final round of the 2010 Masters, Phil Mickelson pulled off one of the riskiest—and most rewarding—shots in major championship history.

But as courageous as Mickelson can be, he also knows how to plan for his misses. Some of the time. In that same Masters, with his lead having been trimmed to two shots after Lee Westwood birdied the 17th hole, Mickelson chose to hit a 3-wood off the tee on the par-4 finishing hole, an uphill, dogleg right. Hitting driver would've put many different scenarios into play, mostly bad—not to mention that Lefty had gotten a little loose with his driver earlier on the back nine. So he eased off the throttle and hit 3-wood to take the fairway bunkers out of play. It was a smart move: His tee shot drifted a little left into the first cut of rough, a safe distance from the bunkers. (Had he hit driver, his tee shot would've certainly found the bunkers.) From there, he hit a 7-iron to 10 feet for birdie to seal his third Masters title and green jacket.

Afterwards, Mickelson credited his ability to overcome mistakes on the 9th, 10th and 11th holes as a big reason why he was able to prevail. He found the woods with his tee shots on all three holes, yet he still managed to get up and down for pars.

"I hit a lot of great shots and [drove] the ball very well, but I made some bad swings on 9, 10 and 11 and I was able to salvage par," said Mickelson. "I was able to get the ball, advance it far enough down by the green where my short game could take over and salvage par. That's why I feel so comfortable here and I'm relaxed when I drive down Magnolia Lane, because I know that I don't have to play perfect golf."

Mickelson hit just seven of 14 fairways during the final round, but he still managed to shoot 5-under par. Ironically, he also shot a 67 in the first round hitting just six of 14 fairways. Mickelson's errant tee shots weren't too bad because he was still able to hit 13 and 14 greens in regulation, respectively, during those two rounds. That's managing your misses.

Reduce the Number of Barrels in Your Ball-flight Rifle

If misses are expected, then obviously the extent and direction of the miss matters. Tour players not only plan and play for their misses, they also train like champions to improve the extent and predictability of their misses. I like to put it this way—if one's ball-flight was analogous to a bullet shot from a rifle, even Tour players are not shooting a gun with one barrel. They can't simply select a target and aim their barrel (their golf shot) at the target and pull the trigger. The ball just doesn't always go where their rifle is aimed. However, it does go pretty close.

Tour players strive to play golf within what I refer to as a "two-barrel rifle"—one barrel aimed where they intend to hit the shot, and the other aimed where they could potentially miss it—expecting the ball to end up somewhere between the two. For example, if a PGA Tour player has a tendency to block his tee shots to the right, he aims his "intended" barrel down the left center of the fairway, so that if the ball comes out of the "blocked right" barrel, the worst case is he ends up in the right rough, not out-of-bounds.

"[Golf] is a game of misses," said the great Ben Hogan. "The guy who misses the best is going to win." Unfortunately, for those of us mere mortals, we don't have the same quality rifle (ball-flight) as a Ben Hogan. In fact, many of us are playing with rifles that have four, five, or six barrels. Ouch! How do you aim a rifle that could send a bullet flying in six different directions? That's exactly the point. It's one thing to play for your misses, but doing so implies that your misses are somewhat predictable and to an extent that they are within play.

Novice golfers can relate well to this idea of having a rifle with too many barrels. They hit one shot perfectly, but then top one, slice one, chunk one, pull one, and pop one up. Instructing them to play their miss creates quite a dilemma—for which miss do they play?

The best one can do is attempt to aim their rifle in a direction that accommodates as many misses as possible (or consider selecting a club that eliminates a barrel or two). The best solution to the six-barrel dilemma is clear—eliminate some barrels. How? As we've discussed throughout this book, hire a coach, practice, and develop your skills. As you do, you will reduce the number of barrels in your "ball-flight rifle" and thus be able to plan and play for your misses.

"Golf is not just a game of great shots, it's a game of bad shots, too," wrote LPGA Hall of Famer Annika Sorenstam in her book, *Golf Annika's Way.* "The champions are the ones who hit the fewest bad shots and are smart enough to keep their bad shots from being terrible."

Sorenstam, whose course management skills are well renowned, had a few simple rules she lived by: 1) If she wasn't 100 percent sure she could hit a particular shot six out of 10 times, she wouldn't try it; and 2) she only allowed herself one risk per hole. If she "went for it" with her tee shot and drove the ball into trouble, she would pitch the ball back into play rather than try and make up a shot. "When in doubt, play it safe," wrote Sorenstam. "You'll save a couple of shots per round."

Summary

1. Recognize that you will not hit every shot where you'd like. You are going to miss shots; the key is to keep those misses playable.
2. In preparing to hit a shot, plan for your miss. If your tendency is to fade the ball, and the pin is tucked up against a massive bunker on the right-hand side of the green, don't go shooting directly at the flag. Give yourself some margin for error and aim 10-20 yards left of the flag, so the ball can fade toward the middle of the green.
3. Consider the consequences. Make sure to aim your shots in a direction in which a miss doesn't cost you an immediate stroke or two (e.g., out of bounds, water hazard, unplayable lies). The key to shooting low scores is eliminating the dreaded double and triple bogeys caused by misses that do not give you a chance to recover.
4. Finally, reduce the number of barrels in your "ball-flight" rifle. Heed the advice presented in earlier chapters—get fit, hire a coach, identify the skills that cost you the most shots, stick with one approach, and walk your skills up the four steps to mastery.

Afterword
EASIER SAID THAN DONE

As you've noticed throughout this book, I've criticized the profession within which I've participated and made a living for most of my career. I've expressed concern for teaching malpractice, recommended coaching over lessons, and explained why I feel that the golf teaching industry is broken. This is not to say that teaching professionals aren't well-intentioned. They are! The vast majority of teachers that I know are hard-working, thoughtful, motivated, passionate students of the game. They are committed to helping you play better golf, and they believe in their hearts that what they are doing makes a difference.

However, these professionals remain confined by a well-entrenched, traditional teaching paradigm that has significant limitations. I can relate all too well. I am as guilty as any of them at conforming to the existing system, taking the easy route, and delivering a product to students that is not what it should be. Unfortunately, doing so is easy to do when other providers offer nothing better, when golfers are uninformed, and when the public doesn't expect or demand anything more.

Early in my career, I worked as a golf instructor. I've engaged in many, if not all, of the same flawed processes that I've noted in this book. Why do you think I'm so familiar with them? Although I've become more educated, knowledgeable, and experienced, I continue to struggle with providing a better alternative for golfers looking to learn the game and to play to their potential. Thus, I personally know that it is "Easier Said Than Done."

It is easier to criticize what's wrong with something than it is to fix it and make it right. It's easier to throw stones (even when you live in the same neighborhood of glass houses), then it is to move away and build a new neighborhood. Yet, there comes a time when we each need to stop behaving like sheep, step out of the flock, and decide to lead. Hopefully, this book will enlighten and motivate you, your teachers, and other professionals to take the lead and pursue a better way of learning and playing the game of golf. For me, writing this book has done just that.

There is progress being made. There are coaches and players across the world who "get it." These trailblazers are reading this book and saying, "What's the big deal—I'm already doing that!" Some teachers currently offer formalized coaching programs and others do operate more like coaches than teachers (even if they do it in the context of lessons). There are also players out there who demand more than quick fixes and have committed the time and resources necessary to truly get better. You can do the same.

As you reviewed each of the 12 Truths, you likely identified with one or two of them. Possibly you realized that you were skipping critical steps in the learning process, or that you've never stuck to something long enough to master it, or that your weakest link was breaking down under pressure. Maybe you made a resolution to start practicing, to approach your rounds with more realistic expectations, or to learn to play with your most familiar ball-flight without tinkering with your swing throughout an entire round.

When you put down this book, you don't need to change your entire approach to the game in one fell swoop. Instead, jot down one or two things that you will do differently moving forward. Don't stop at simply "knowing" the 12 Truths; instead, do as the pros do—apply them!

If you've been pursuing the self-help route and never had a golf lesson, hire a coach and you may surprise yourself at how fast you'll improve. If you currently have a teacher, sit down and discuss what it would take for you to really get better. Create and commit to a cost-effective coaching arrangement that focuses on building your skill (not just your swing) while opening the door to those tour-tested strategies used on the PGA and LPGA tours (as well as most other sports)—a focus on fitness, supervised practice, transfer training, and on-course coaching.

Now that you know what it takes to play to your potential on the golf course, you must demand it from those in the golf teaching industry. You've heard of the economic model of "supply and demand"—well, once an informed golfing public demands better coaching, the industry will provide it. If, however, golfers continue living in denial and demanding quick fixes, little will change!

Fortunately, you control your own destiny. You do not have to follow the flock of wishful thinkers looking for the quick fix. You, alone, can decide to put in the time and energy to improve your game once and for all.

Yes, the 12 Truths are "Easier Said Than Done"—this explains why everyone doesn't do them! The few that do, get ahead. Those who demonstrate the ability to walk the talk, to implement, to apply the 12 Truths rise to the top. This disciplined execution is what separates the best from the rest. I invite you to stop talking and start doing. Become one of the few who actually do the things that are "Easier Said Than Done."

"The most rewarding things you do in life are often the ones that look like they cannot be done." –Arnold Palmer